# GLOBALISING PROFESSIONAL EDUCATION IN INDIA

# GLOBALISING PROFESSIONAL EDUCATION IN INDIA

*Editor*

**V.C. Pandey**

ISHA

**ISHA BOOKS**

**DELHI-110033**

Globalising Professional Education in India

ISBN: 81-8205-357-9

Rs. 690



Published in 2006 in India by
Isha Books
D-43, Prithviraj Road, Adarsh Nagar, Delhi-110033
E-mail : ishabooks@hotmail.com

*Laser Typesetting at:* Master Computers, New Delhi
*Printed at:* Salasar Imaging System, Delhi

# Contents

# Preface

This book aims at providing an acccount on how Education system has undergone a sea change over the years and brought tremendous improvement in various fields. At the same time the process of globalisation and liberalisation has created a system that has fostered inequality and motivated society to act on social security front while coping with new challenges and contradictions.

This book contains eleven chapters dealing with various issues having beginning in the past and have relevance even today. The first chapter "Design and Strategy of Promoting Professional Education"–Scans the various Education–Policies, a recommendations of commissions on education as to how the curriculum should be prepared taking view of needs of all sections of society and how the Constitutional provisions should be followed while implementing such programmes.

The chapter two "Universalization of Secondary Education"–takes into consideration the broader perspective of providing education to all–as has been mentioned under the Directive Principles of the State Policy. 'Curriculum methods and Instructional Strategies' goes into detail on how the curriculum methods should be followed and at the practical level discharged for greater impact and results.

'Mobility and Motivation' factors undertakes a comparative study of allowances and benefits in a bigger as well as smaller organisations and their impact on the performance of individuals. How such benefits as motives lead to emigration and later better earning capacity.

'Life Style Related Issues, and Work Environment' deliberate upon how the process of globalisation and marketisation has created opportunities for all and simultaneously, created inequality. As a result, more attention has been given to social and economic security concerns and for that various types of allowances and programmes being initiated by the World Bank since 1980's.

'Education of Children' considers children as the most vulnerable section of society subject to delinquency, generation gap negative onslaught on their character by media than their contribution. In such a given situation institutions line the school, family and the society at large–find themselves in quandary how to prepare a curriculum that works as panacea for all ills.

'Old Age Settlement Problems and Issues, related to social security ponders over social security both as a concept and as a system. It views both the organized and the unorganized sectors where the society takes social security measures for its member related to maternity, unemployment, Old Age and Death. A comparative study of amount spent on such measures in various countries of their GDP in relation to India has been mentioned.

'Transformation of India into an Advanced Nation' undertakes the role of universities in producing professionals and how these institutions should be further equipped with modern paraphernalia AIIMS, IITS, IIMS, and various regional institutions contribute their valuable service but still our traditional sectors are not being paid proper attention. So our institutions should churn out such professionals who can help adopt new technologies to our traditional needs, challenges of globalisation and cope with the necessities of a welfare states.

'Innovative Professional Development' reflects upon the role of universities nowadays in providing new courses fulfilling needs of the present market economy. DRTC, AIIMS, IITS, IIMS, UGC and a host of private institutions fulfilling such demands.

'Life style and related diseases'– under this chapter a co-relation between education and consequent life style has been established. More educated persons are less vulnerable to fatal diseases like AIDS.

The Consequence of Global Education stress on the need for more education that in turn faster much economic growth and later this will also lead to reduction of all forms of inequality and bring about desired political change.

**Editor**

# 1

# Design and Strategy of Promoting Professional Education

Educational policy and progress have been reviewed in the light of the goal of national development and priorities set from time to time. In its Resolution on the National Policy on Education in 1968, an emphasis on quality improvement and a planned, more equitable expansion of educational facilities and the need to focus on the education of girls was stressed. About a decade ago and a half later, the National Policy on Education (NPE-1986) was formulated which was further updated in 1992.

The NPE 1986 provides for a comprehensive policy framework for the development of education upto the end of the century and a Plan of Action (POA) 1992, assigning specific responsibilities for organising, implementing and financing its proposals. India's commitment to the spread of knowledge and freedom of thought among its citizens is reflected in its Constitution. The Directive Principle contained in Article 45 enjoins that "the State shall endeavour to provide within a period of ten years from the commencement of this Constitution, for free and compulsory education for all children until they complete the age of fourteen years".

Article 29 (i) provides that any citizen having a distinct language, script, special care of the economic and educational interests of the underprivileged sections, particularly, the Scheduled Castes and Scheduled Tribes is laid down as an obligation of the State under article 46. Though education is in the concurrent list of the Constitution, the State Governments play a very major role in the development of education particularly in the primary and the secondary education sectors.

## Structure and Progress of Education

The focus in on the broad dimensions and magnitude of the structure, organisation and progress in education. Further it also highlights growth and priority areas in education in India that point to the challenges of the future. There are about 888 thousands educational institutions in the country with an enrolment of about 179 millions. Elementary Education System in India is the second largest in the World with 149.4 millions children of 6-14 years enrolled and 2.9 million teachers. This is about 82% of the children in the age group.

A uniform structure of school education, the 10+2 system has been adopted by all the States and Union Territories of India. However, within the States and the UTs, there remains variations in the number of classes constituting the Primary, Upper Primary, High and Higher Secondary school stages, age for admission to class I, medium of instruction, public examinations, teaching of Hindi and English, number of working days in a year, academic session, vacation periods, fee structure, compulsory education etc.

### *Different Stages of Education*

The Primary Stage consists of Classes I-V, i.e., of five years duration, in 20 States/UTs namely Andhra Pradesh, Arunachal Pradesh, Bihar, Haryana, Himachal Pradesh, Jammu & Kashmir, Madhya Pradesh, Manipur, Orissa,

Punjab, Rajasthan, Sikkim, Tamil Nadu, Tripura, Uttar Pradesh, West Bengal, Andaman & Nicobar Islands, Chandigarh, Delhi and Karaikal and Yanam regions of Pondicherry. The primary stage consists of classes I-IV in Assam, Goa, Gujarat, Karnataka, Kerala, Maharashtra, Meghalaya, Mizoram, Nagaland, Dadra & Nagar Haveli, Daman & Diu, Lakshadweep and Mahe region of Pondicherry

The Middle Stage of education comprises Classes VI-VIII in as many as 18 States.Uts viz., Arunachal Pradesh, Bihar, Haryana, Himachal Pradesh, Jammu & Kashmir, Madhya Pradesh, Manipur, Punjab, Rajasthan, Sikkim, Tamil Nadu, Tripura, Uttar Pradesh, West Bengal, Andaman & Nicobar Islands, Chandigarh, Delhi and Karaikal region of Pondicherry; Classes V-VII in Assam, Goa, Gujarat, Karnataka, Kerala, Maharashtra, Meghalaya, Mizoram, Dadra & Nagar Haveli, Daman & Diu, Lakshadweep and Mahe region of Pondicherry and Classes VI-VII in Andhra Pradesh, Orissa and Yanam region of Pondicherry. In Nagaland Classes V - VIII constitute the upper primary stage.

The Secondary Stage consists of Classes IX-X in 19 States/UTs. Viz., Arunachal Pradesh, Bihar, Haryana, Himachal Pradesh, Jammu & Kashmir, Madhya Pradesh, Manipur, Nagaland, Punjab, Rajasthan, Sikkim, Tamil Nadu, Tripura, Uttar Pradesh, West Bengal, Andaman & Nicobar Islands, Chandigarh, Delhi and Karaikal region of Pondicherry. The High School stage comprises classes VIII to X in 13 States/UTs viz., Andhra Pradesh, Assam, Goa, Gujarat, Karnataka, Kerala, Maharashtra, Meghalaya, Mizoram, Orissa, Dadra & Nagar Haveli, Daman & Diu, Lakshadweep and Mahe & Yanam regions of Pondicherry. However, the Higher Secondary / Senior Secondary stage of school comprising classes XI-XII (10+2 pattern) is available in all the States/UTs though in some States/UTs these classes are attached to Universities/Colleges.

The minimum age for admission to class I of the Primary School stage is generally 5+ or 6+ years. In 22 States/UTs the minimum age for admission to Class I is 5+ years and in 7 States/UTs the minimum age for admission is 6+ years. There is no age restriction in the case of Mizoram. In Gujarat, the minimum age for admission is 5+ years (voluntary) and 6+ years (compulsory). In Lakshadweep, the minimum age for admission is 5 ½ years.

### Language Teaching

Mother tongue or regional language is the medium of instruction at the primary stage of education in most of the States/UTs. Facilities for studying in a medium other than regional language vary considerable in different States and Union Territories.

Apart from Hindi speaking States, teaching of Hindi is compulsory in most of the non-Hindi speaking States/UTs, though the classes from which the teaching of Hindi is compulsory differ from State to State. Teaching of Hindi is not compulsory in the States of Tamil Nadu, Tripura and Karaikal region of Pondicherry.

Teaching of English is compulsory in all the States/UTs, except Bihar. However, the classes in which teaching of English is compulsory differs from State to State. In general, it is compulsory in Classes VI-X in most of the States/UTs.

### Public Examinations

In all the States/UTs Public Examinations are conducted at the end of X an XII Classes by the respective State Boards of Secondary and Higher Secondary Education. The minimum age for the Secondary School Examination varies from 14+ to 16+ years in Andhra Pradesh, Arunachal Pradesh, Assam, Bihar, Gujarat, Jammu & Kashmir, Karnataka, Kerala, Maharashtra, Manipur, Orissa, Punjab, Tamil Nadu,

Tripura, West Bengal, Andaman & Nicobar Islands, Delhi, Lakshadweep and Pondicherry.

In Mizoram, the minimum age for secondary school examination is 13+ years. Other States/UTs either do not have age restriction or have not prescribed any age restriction. The minimum age for higher Secondary School Examination varies from 16+ to 18+ years in Arunachal Pradesh, Bihar, Gujarat, Jammu & Kashmir, Kerala, Maharashtra, Punjab, Tamil Nadu, Tripura, Andaman & Nicobar Islands, Delhi, Lakshadweep and Pondicherry. In other States/UTs, either there is no age restriction prescribed or if it exists, it has not been indicated. In some of the States/UTs, the first Public Examination is also conducted at the Middle stage of School Education. The number of working days of School Education in a year is generally more than 200 days in all the States/UTs.

***Compulsory Education***

Compulsory education has been enforced in four States and Union Territories at the primary stage of education while in eight States/UTs there is compulsory education covering the entire elementary stage of education. As many as 20 States/UTs have not introduced any measure of compulsion upto the year 1997-98.

***Free Education***

A majority of States and Union Territories have introduced free education in Classes I-XII of their schools. In the States/UTs where education is not free for classes IX and above, the annual fee varies considerably from the highest level of Rs. 360/- for classes XI and XII in the case of Meghalaya to the lowest at Rs. 48/- in the case of Assam.

From 1968 onwards, goal has been to set apart 6% of National Income on education. In spite of resource constraints as well as competing priorities, the Budgetary expenditure on education by Centre & States as percentage of Gross National Product has steadily increased from 0.8% in 1951-52 to 3.3% in 1994-95.

Para 11.4 of NPE, 1986 states "that the investment on education be gradually increased to reach a level of 6% of the National Income as early as possible. Since the actual level of investment has remained far short of that target, it is important that greater determination is shown now to find the funds for the programmes laid down in this policy. While actual requirements will be computed from time to time on the basis of monitoring and review, the outlay on education will be stepped up to ensure that during the 8th Five year Plan and onwards it will uniformly exceed 6% of the national income".

The total budgetary expenditure on Education by the Education Departments of the Centre and States has increased from Rs. 644.6 millions in 1951-52 to Rs. 300,000millions in 1995-96. In terms of its share in total budgetary expenditure, it has increased from 7.9% in 1951-52 to 11.1% in 1995-96. There are, at present 130 plan schemes in the Department with a total Eighth Plan outlay of Rs. 74430 Millions. The total plan outlay of the Department for the year 1996-97 is Rs. 33827 millions.

There are 18 Centrally Sponsored Schemes which account for 65.7% of the total plan outlay. Mid-Day-Meal Scheme is the major Centrally Sponsored Scheme with 1996-97 outlay of Rs.14,000 millions. Other major Centrally Sponsored Schemes are Operation Blackboard, Non-formal Education, Teacher Education, Post Literacy and Continuing Education and Vocational Education with 1996-97 Outlay of Rs. 2790 millions, Rs. 1582.5 millions, Rs. 1170 millions, Rs. 755 millions and Rs. 820 millions respectively.

### Engineering Education

Engineering education, unlike other types of professional

education, has not had a long history. Though the ancients and medievals had built large brick and stone houses, castles, cities and huge temples, bad constructed long highways and aqueducts and dug canals, which show considerable knowledge of what are now earned civil and hydraulic engineering and of properties of building materials, this knowledge must have been derived empirically. Beginnings of mechanical engineering are to be found in the manufacture and use, of tools, means of transport, simple machinery like lathes, and weapons of offence and defense. Rudiments of chemical engineering are to be seen in the old metallurgical practices.

But there were no organised schools for teaching apprentices the use of machinery or knowledge of processes; knowledge passed from generation to generation of craftsmen and artificers, by word of mouth, and was thus confined to castes and guilds. The Industrial Revolution With the advent of the Industrial Age, which was ushered in by the discovery of the steam engine by James Watt about 1780, and the ability to, generate and to handlè large amounts of power rendered possible by the invention of the steam engine, men passed from dependence on human labour and hand tools to large and complicated machinery; production of commodities passed from cottage workshops to factories.

Transportation by bullock-carts, horse-driven carriages, and wind or man driven boats, gave way to railroads and steamships. All this necessitated the construction of large machines, engines, ships and carriages, and gave rise to problems of industrial finance and labour. Early Engineering School in Europe-While inventive genius was called upon to devise new kinds of machines and to handle new types of processes, the craftsmen and artisans were called upon to put these designs into actual practice. They were asked to test and handle these machines and to repair them whenever necessary.

The engineer was thus evolved from two different streams- first from the artisans and craftsmen on one side, who belonged to the lower orders of the less specialised society of the last century, and on the other side from the genteel class who had knowledge of sciences, and had acquired habits of disciplined and organised thinking. Sometimes the two types merged in the same person i.e. the craftsman taught himself science, and learnt to think and invent; or the man with scientific definite objective 9.

It was soon found that it was not possible to depend upon unlettered mechanics and craftsmen to manufacture, according to designs given to them, the new types of machines which were constantly coming into use, or upon apprentices to handle these machines properly, unless they were instructed in their use. Schools for general education of craftsmen and artisans, and for teaching apprentices the use of machines were founded by John Anderson at Glasgow about 1790, and Dr. Birkbeck in London in 1823.

The nineteenth century has witnessed the birth of many branches of engineering and technology in addition to the classical ones of civil and mechanical. The range of development in engineering and technology is illustrated by the following lists of separate engineering fields which are recognised and in which four or five years of undergraduate courses leading to a degree are offered in American universities and colleges. Within each one of the fields, there are further sub- divisions and specialisations, each being the subject of special postgraduate study and research.

Technology and engineering are products of fundamental discoveries in basic sciences, and as is well known, these began to accumulate in the late nineteenth and in the twentieth centuries and in greater variety than in all the previous 50 centuries of civilised life. Inventive genius in Europe and America tried to utilise these science for new industries, and for other human needs. Thus new branches of engineering began to grow. To give a few examples:

Electrical engineering which now claims as many as, or more professionals and students than the older branches of civil or mechanical, started actually from the year 1882, when Edison built the first central electric power house to supply electrical power to factories, and light and power for domestic use to dwellers of a city. The discovery of the law of electromagnetic induction was made by Faraday in 1831, but it required work of a half a century to put the discovery to practical use.

With the multiplication of the number of e electrical power houses, and with the long distance transmission of power, the demand for men trained in the use of electrical machinery and acquainted with the fundamentals of the science began to grow, find the universities and technical colleges began to introduce courses in electrical engineering. But only one or two colleges are known to have introduced electrical engineering courses earlier than 1880. So rapid has been the progress in this field that the number of electrical engineers, technicians and craftsmen in the U.S.A. is now estimated to be nearing the million mark.

The same is trite of automotive engineering which dates from the time of the discovery of the internal combustion engine by Otto in 1870. Rudiments of chemical engineering were known in earlier metallurgical practices, but the great discoveries in organic, physical and inorganic chemistry subsequent to 1880, led to more and more large scale chemical industries. Chemical engineering courses began to be introduced about 1890, almost simultaneously in the German Technische Hoschschules and in great American Technical Colleges like the Massachusetts Institute of Technology (M.I.T.). The first courses were introduced in England in the Imperial College of Science and Technology in 1911.

Electrical engineering is a typical example of this change. For about 20 years it dealt mainly with electrical power generation, transmission and utilisation. With Marconi's discovery of wireless telegraphy (1898), electrical engineers began to study and watch the progress of Radio Communication. In some, university and technical colleges, the new science began to be pursued as a subject for post-gradate study and research. Then came the discovery of the use of triode valves in 1914 which revolutionised radio communication, and made broad- casting possible. This led to the need for a large number of engineers trained in the fundamentals of radio communications, and in the use of the necessary appliances. So universities and technical colleges were called upon to open undergraduate classes for the training of radio engineers.

Many developments of electrical engineering have emerged, such as power plant and transmission engineering, radio communication, telephone communication, electronics, electrical calculating machines, electric railway engineering, electrical recording apparatus, electricity and electronics in medicine, and surgery, electrical control apparatus, servo-mechanisms and many others. These subdivisions of the engineering field illustrate how a mature economy develops a great variety of ways for controlling and using the processes and resources of nature. The great productiveness of a country like America is due less to possession of natural resources than to the development of a wide range of skills. Thus three basic types of engineering have developed into numerous new technologies, which have tended to become independent field.

The engineer should be alert for any fundamental discovery winch may be, turned to practical use and for betterment of the processes he is using. The structure of engineering education should be such that when opportunities occur it will be possible for the country or the industries to collect requisite personnel, from technicians to executive engineers, to turn the discovery to use within as short a period as possible. Such a set-up of engineering education existed in Germany, and exists in the U.S.A., but not in the United Kingdom, of which the Indian system was for long a bad and obsolete copy.

Thus though many of the great and fundamental discoveries which led to Radar and Atomic Energy utilisation were made by British physicists, their large scale utilisation was for war purpose was possible only in America, where the requisite personnel of all types could be assembled and set to work. The British recognized this defect in their structure of Engineering and Technological Education during the course of the last way, Their Ministry of Education set up a committee under Lord Eustace Percy "To advise the Ministry on the needs of higher technical education in England and Wales, with particular attention to the means required for maintaining appropriate co-operation between universities and technical colleges."

The impulse for creation of centres of technical training came from the British rulers of India, and it arose out of the necessity for the training of overseers for construction and maintenance of public buildings, roads, canals, and ports, and for the training of artisans and craftsmen for the use of instruments, and apparatus needed for the army, the navy, and the survey department. The superintending engineers were mostly recruited from Britain from the Cooper's Hill College, and this applied as well to foremen and artificers; but this could not be done in the case of lower grades-craftsmen, artisans and sub-overseers who were recruited locally. As they were mostly illiterate, efficiency was low.

The necessity to make them more efficient by giving them elementary lessons in reading, writing, arithmetic, geometry, and mechanics, led to the establishment of industrial schools attached to Ordnance Factories and other engineering establishments. While it is stated that such schools existed in Calcutta and Bombay as early as 1825,

Madras, in 1842, attached to the Gun Carriage Factory there. A school for the training of overseers was known to exist in Poona in 1854.

Meanwhile in Europe and America, Colleges of Engineering were growing up, which drew to them men having good education, and special proficiency in mathematical subjects. This led to discussions in Government circles in India, and similar institutions were sought to be established in the Presidency Towns. The first engineering college was established in the U.P. in 1847 for the training of Civil Engineers at Roorkee, which made use of the large workshops and public buildings there that were erected for the Upper Ganges Canal.

The Roorkee College (or to give it its official name, the Thomason Engineering College) was never affiliated to any university, but has been giving diplomas which are considered to be equivalent to degrees. In pursuance of the Government policy, three Engineering Colleges were opened by about 1856 in the three Presidencies. In Bengal, a College called the Calcutta College of Civil Engineering was opened at the Writers' Buildings in November 1856; the name was changed to Bengal Engineering College in 1857, and it, was affiliated to the Calcutta University. It gave a licentiate course in Civil Engineering.

In 1865 it was amalgamated with the Presidency College. Later, in 1880, it was detached from the Presidency College and shifted to its present quarters at Sibpur, occupy in the premises and buildings belonging to the Bishop's College. Proposals for having an Engineering College at Bombay city having failed for some reasons, the overseers' school at Poona eventually became the Poona College of Engineering and affiliated to the Bombay University in 1858. For a long time, this was the only College of Engineering in the Western Presidency.

In the Madras Presidency, the industrial school attached to the Gun Carriage Factory became ultimately the

Guindy College of Engineering and affiliated to the Madras University (1858). The educational work in the three Colleges of Sibpur, Poona, and Guindy has been more or less similar. They all had licentiate courses in civil engineering up to 1880, when they organised degree classes in this branch alone. After 1880, the demand for mechanical and electrical engineering was felt, but the three Engineering Colleges started only apprenticeship classes in these subjects.

The Victoria Jubilee Technical Institute, which was started at Bombay in 1887, had as its objective the training of licentiates in Electrical, Mechanical and Textile Engineering. In 1915, the Indian Institute of Science, Bangalore, opened Electrical Engineering classes under Dr. Alfred Hay, and began to give certificates and associateships, the latter being regarded equivalent to a degree. In Bengal, the leaders of the Swadeshi Movement organised in 1907 a National Council of Education which tried to organise a truly National University. Out of the many institutions it started, only the College of Engineering and Technology at Jadavpur had survived. It started granting diplomas in a mechanical and engineering course in 1908, and in chemical engineering in 1921.

The Calcutta University Commission, debated the pros and cons for the introduction of degree courses in mechanical and electrical engineering. One of the reasons cited, form the recommendations of the Indian Industrial Commission against the introduction of electrical engineering courses is given in the following quotation from their report: "We have not specifically referred to the training of electrical engineers, because electrical manufactures have not yet been started in India, and there is only scope for the employment of men to do simple repair work, to take charge of the running of electrical machinery, and to manage and control hydroelectric and steam-operated stations.

The men required for these three classes of work will be provided by the foregoing proposals for the training of the various grades required in mechanical engineering. They will have to acquire in addition, special experience in electrical matters, but, till this branch of engineering is developed on the constructional side, and the manufacture of electrical machinery taken in hand, the managers of electrical undertakings must train their own men, making such use as they can of the special facilities offered for instruction at the engineering colleges and the Indian Institute of Science".

The credit of first starting degree classes in mechanical and electrical engineering and in metallurgy belong to the University of Banaras. About fifteen years later, in 1931-32, the Bengal Engineering College at Sibpur started mechanical engineering courses, electrical engineering courses in 1935-36, and courses in metallurgy in 1939-40. Courses in these subjects were also introduced at Guindy and Poona about the same time. Quite a number of engineering colleges have been started since August 15, 1947. It is due to the realisation that India has to be come a great industrial country, and would require a far larger number of engineers than could be supplied by the older institutions. In some cases, existing lower type institutions have been raised to the status of degree-giving colleges.

The last half of this century has transformed our environment, perhaps radically, and brought more changes in our lives and thinking than in any corresponding period in history. These are the consequences of discoveries of sciences and applications of technology. The concept of absolute knowledge in the sense of storing all knowledge is perhaps no more relevant today. Our efforts for reconciling the traditional concepts and ways with the demands of technological age cannot provide simple solutions for our difficulties and complexities based on such stored knowledge. Frontiers of knowledge are themselves expanding rapidly making it possible to device newer and more efficient methods of solving problems of the society.

Education must therefore make efforts for securing knowledge and mastering modern skills and methods than merely storing and distributing the traditional ones. For this purpose of training of mind and mastering of skills and for harnessing science and technology to profitable and productive processes of economic growth and social well-being, the technological education system has to be continuously reviewed and adopted. This has indeed been the basis of our efforts during the last three decades, the result is that there is a well-organised structure and a wide network of technical institutions offering different types of programmes: craftsman courses, technician (diploma) courses, graduate and post- graduate courses, etc., catering to the various levels of knowledge, skills and competences required by the economy.

## Craftsmen Courses

Training is imparted in 32 Engineering and 22 non-engineering trades approved by the National Council for Training in Vocational Trades to young people within the age group of 15 to 25 years. For this purpose 357 Industrial Training Institutes with an overall capacity of 1,55,000 training places have been established in the various parts of the country. Period of training ranges from 1 year to 2 years. The Industrial Training Institutes are also used as Basic Training Centres for the Apprenticeship Training Programmes under the Apprentices Act 1961.

The 103 trades designated under the Apprentices Act follow our national classification of occupations and cover 216 industries. There are seven Central Training Institutes for training of Instructors under the Directorate General of Employment and Training. These Institutes conduct regular, refresher and retraining programmes for the Craft

Instructors in various engineering and non-engineering trades.

The Instructor- trainees are deputed mostly by the various Industrial Training Institutes and Industrial Establishments in the country. At the end of the last decade, it was realised that higher or advanced levels of skills were required by the industry both in Public and Private sectors for working on the more modern and highly specialised type of machine tools and equipment coming to be used extensively. To meet this need the following institutes have been established:-

a) Advanced Training Institute, Madras-The advanced Training Institute, Madras, imparts training in Advanced Vocational skills such as Tool Design, Tool and Die-Making, Heat Treatment, Metallurgy, Machine Tool Maintenance and Advanced Welding etc.

b) Foreman Training Institute, Bangalore - The Foreman Training Institute, Bangalore imparts training not only in developing further skills but also in managerial skills for first line supervisors.

c) Central Staff Training and Research Institute, Calcutta-The Central Staff Training and Research Institute set up at Calcutta is charged with the responsibility of conducting training programmes for officers and staff of the Central and State Governments and from industry, who control, regulate and direct Vocational and Apprenticeship Training Programmes. This Institute is also involved in the Research and Developmental activities in the field of vocational Training.

d) Advanced Training Institute in Electronics, Hyderabad-The Advanced Training Institute in Electronics, Hyderabad, has been set up last year to provide training at Craftsmen and Technician level for the electronic personnel required in the country.

## Technician Cources

### *Post-Matric Technical Education*

Diploma level courses for the training of middle level man power needed for a wide range of professional duties, for application of knowledge in field operation, in production and construction, testing and development etc., and such functions are offered in 291 polytechnics with an annual enrolment capacity of about 50,000 students. They offer a variety of specialization in engineering and technology as well as in a few non- technological fields. The courses are normally of three years duration where full-time institutional instruction is offered and 31/2 to 4 years when instruction is on a Sandwich or on part-time basis.

Recently a number of diversified courses and facilities for evening part-time education have also been provided in some polytechnics situated in metropolitan cities where the demand for such courses exists. About two dozen Women Polytechnics with courses of special interest to, and employment potential for, women, have also been established, particularly to cater to the needs of the socially/ economically inhibited classes who might be reluctant to take advantage of the facilities generally available in the regular polytechnics. The products of the diploma courses are expected to take up supervisory positions in field and industry.

## Degree Level Education

Degree level-For the professional engineers and technologists, facilities for technical education are available in 141 engineering colleges offering courses leading to the award of Bachelor Degree in Engineering and Technology. The total admission capacity annually for these courses is of the order of 25,000. The duration of most of these degree courses is five years and with the new pattern of Secondary

Education of 10+2, it is expected to change over completely by 1981-82 to a duration of four years.

## Post-Graduate Courses

For the benefit of those who have higher level academic achievements as also for under taking research and development activities in engineering and technology, post-graduate courses have been offered widely in the various selected institutions offering degree courses. The number of the institutions offering such post-graduate courses is 65 with an annual intake capacity of about 2,000. These courses normally lead to the Master's Degree in the concerned discipline and are of two years duration. Facilities also exist at these centres offering part-time courses at the Post-graduate level for those who are already in service. Duration of such courses normally is three years.

## Management Education

Any effort at improvement of the utilisation of available resources and maximisation of results has necessarily to take into account better concepts of management and organisational development of the system as a whole. With this in view a chain of institutions numbering about 30 mostly in the University sector offering management courses both at the First Degree and Advanced levels has been started. The courses offered at the various institutions to date cover training at the Master's Degree level for the M.B.A. degree with an annual admission capacity of about, 1000.

The Vocational Training/Craftsmen Courses are offered at the Industrial Training Institutes. The Diploma courses are offered in the Polytechnics which are widely spread over all the States and Union Territories and are affiliated to the respective State Boards of Technical Education who lay down in general the levels and standards of the courses and guide the system of evaluation of the students appearing at the examination. Degree and Post-Graduate courses are offered in colleges affiliated to the various Universities, certain University Departments, and institutions declared as of national importance or as deemed Universities.

### *Indian Institutes of Technology*

These are our apex institutions for engineering education and research. Each Institute conducts a First degree course and Master's Degree course in a wide range of subject fields, and also offers facilities for Research and Doctoral work. The main emphasis at the Institutes is on the Post-Graduate studies and Research with an inter-disciplinary approach. To this end each Institute has developed good departments of Physics, Chemistry, Mathematics, and Social Sciences which inter-act with the departments of Engineering and Technology.

The student enrolment at the Institutes at the Undergraduate level is limited to 1250 and admission at the Post-Graduate level is designedly kept at about the same order as in the under-graduate courses. The Institutes are in various stages of consolidation and development. As part of the national plan of science and technology, five Centres of Advanced Study and Research have been set up in the Indian Institutes of Technology in Energy Studies (Delhi), Material Science (Kanpur), Cryogenic Engineering (Kharagpur), Ocean Engineering (Madras) and Resource Engineering (Bombay).

### *Indian Institute of Science, Bangalore*

The Indian Institute of Science, Bangalore the oldest and leading post-graduate and research centre in Science and Engineering has facilities in special fields which include Electronics and Communication Engineering, Aeronautical Engineering, Heat and Power Engineering, High Voltage

Engineering, Power Engineering, Bio-Chemistry, Chemistry, Physics and Mathematics. A major Centre in Automation and Control Systems and another in Electronics Design Technology are in the process of establishment.

### *Regional Engineering Colleges*

Fifteen Regional Engineering Colleges have been established in various States as a joint and co- operative enterprise of the Central and the State Governments concerned. Each Engineering College is functioning as an all-India institution admitting students and recruiting faculty from all parts of the country. Fifty percent of the admissions of these institutions (each of which is being equipped for a total annual students intake of 250) is reserved for students from the other States than the ones in which they are located.

In addition to the under-graduate courses these Colleges (which are academically affiliated to the Universities in the respective regions and administratively autonomous being managed by Board of Governors) also offer Post-graduate courses in various subject fields. Special feature of some of these institutions are the industrially oriented Postgraduate courses in Engineering and Technology to train specialist Engineers for Design, Construction and Production work.

### *State Colleges and University Departments*

In addition to the above institutions offering courses at degree and post-graduate level, there is a wide net work of engineering colleges established and administered by the State Governments, Universities and private agencies; they are also affiliated to the respective Universities, and offer degree courses in a variety of subject fields. Some of them are more than a century old and have been pioneers in engineering education in the country. Many of these State colleges and University Departments are making significant contribution in the field of technical education.

***Special Institutions***

In additions to the above institutions there are certain specialised institutions which offer education/training in specific fields-

*Indian institutes of management*: Three Institutes of Management have been established at Ahmedabad, Calcutta and Bangalore. Ahemdabad, and Calcutta Institutes were established quite some time ago and the Bangalore Institute has just graduated its second batch of full time students for the M.B.A. programme. These Institutes, in addition to the offering of the M.B.A. courses at pre-employment stage for fresh University graduates, offer advanced fellowship programmes in various areas of their specialisation. They also conduct a number of in-service Executive Development Programmes and are concentrating on different sectors of the economy such as Rural Development, Energy, Transportation, etc.

National Institute for Training in Industrial Engineering, Bombay offers a two years post-graduate programme in Industrial Engineering as also a number of Executive Development Programmes and Unit based programmes in various areas of specific interest to specific employing agencies. National Institute of Foundry and Forge Technology, Ranchi - offers a special post-graduate training programme of 12-18 months duration in Advanced Foundry and Forge techniques for personnel from the industry. Indian School of Mines, Dhanbad - which has been declared a deemed University is a specialised Centre for Undergraduate and Post- graduate studies and research in Mining, Applied Geology, Petroleum Technology and Geo-Physics. Technical Teacher's Training Institutes at Bhopal, Calcutta, Chandigarh and Madras offer special 'training' to serving teachers of polytechnics.

There are also other institutions offering courses in architecture and town planning (such as School of Planning and Architecture at New Delhi which offers degree course in Architecture and Post-graduate course in Town Planning with specialisation in Urban Design, Housing and Community Planning, Transportation and Traffic Engineering). Sugar Technology. (National Institute of Sugar Technology, Kanpur), Food Technology Industrial Design (National Institute of Industrial Design, Ahmedabad), Marine Engineering (College of Marine Engineering, Bombay), etc.

By the end of the Third Plan in 1966, most of the above institutions had been started and it was considered necessary to Jay special emphasis thereafter on consolidation and development of the facilities rather than on setting up of additional institutions. Accordingly a special scheme of Quality Improvement was launched for raising the standards of instruction/training at these institutions. The measures under the Quality Improvement programme included the development of faculty, revision and improvement of curriculum including laboratory practices, and schemes for industrial training and refresher courses for the teachers.

Facilities are provided at 14 Centres including the I.I.Ts, Roorkee University, and the Indian Institute of Science, Bangalore for enrolling serving teachers sponsored by the various institutions/agencies for Master's Degree and Doctorate Degree programmes. In this effort of updating and upgrading the level and standard of the faculty, provision was also made for appropriate industrial training for periods of 1-3 months. Short-term and Winter Schools offering special orientation courses, refresher courses etc., were also organised both at these advanced centres and others wherever facilities could be identified and organised.

So far about 26,000 teachers have taken part in these programmes. Curriculum Development Centres were also set up in respect of the various branches of Engineering and Technology to update the curriculum at the under-graduate level in consultation with the users of the institutional products. These Curriculum Development Centres have also engaged them selves in developing concepts for laboratory lay-out, workshop practice etc.

On a similar analogy of the teachers for degree level institutions, considerable efforts have also gone in for the training of teachers for the technician courses. Because of the large number involved and the specialised training required it was considered to have a specific institutional frame work for this type of programme and accordingly four regional institutions were started for this purpose. These Technical Teacher's Training Institutes at Bhopal, Calcutta, Chandigarh and Madras have been offering a regular two-years course for serving teachers from the polytechnics in the respective regions. This two year programme consists of updating of subjects of the concerned teachers, industrial training and pedagogic training. In addition to these specific programmes, these institutes have also done work in areas of curriculum development, Short-term courses, refresher courses, production of teaching materials and textbooks etc.

### *Apprenticeship Training Programme*

With the sparsely distributed and relatively under-developed industrial base in the country and with a large number of technical institutions having been situated not within the easy access of industrial establishments, it was not possible in the earlier years of planning to arrange for in- industry training of all technical students. Nonetheless it was recognised and it is imperative that the institutional training should be supplemented with appropriate field/ industrial training for adequate practical exposure to practical experience. With this end in view a practical training stipends scheme was operated in a limited way in cooperation with the then existing industrial establishments.

Later on, however, a massive apprenticeship training programme was introduced in 1962 for the vocational Training level and in 1974 for the Diploma and Degree levels under the Apprentices Act, 1961 as amended. While for the craftsmen course, training is provided within the course framework, the training at the degree and diploma level is provided after the institutional courses for the duration of a year. This is expected to be both an extension of the educational process as also a preparation of the candidates for later employment.

## Continuing Education

Recognising that opportunities for technical education might have been denied to some on various considerations of economic/ income constraint and other factors, efforts are being made to provide for a vertical advancement of the personnel from one level of a technical education/training to the next higher one. Thus a worker with a National Trade/Apprenticeship Certificate, can take on a diploma course and similarly facilities for some who have a proven ability for academic achievement might go for specialty designed degree courses in some of the institutions.

Availability of part-time courses, evening courses, etc., in certain of the Centres also provides for this vertical mobility. These are, however, offered at present on a limited scale and within the structure of diploma/degree courses. Part-time post-graduate courses for serving engineers also cater to those who are desirous of these facilities at higher levels.

Significant as the achievements in creating facilities for technical education in the country over the last three decades are, there appears a good need now for total review of the system that has been built up, with a view to make it more relevant and effective to the national needs. For historical reasons, the technical education system has been more or less inward looking: the impact of the system on the other elements of the economy is yet to be objectively assessed. The professional engineer or technologist is not a solitary individual unconnected with the happenings in the other spheres of the system.

Of immediate concern, perhaps, for the professionals is, no doubt, the chosen field of his profession but the interaction with the allied professionals, as also the neighbouring community has also to be taken into account to determine the professionals, place in the whole system.

To take first the building of the competence of the professional itself, we might try to understand the efficiency with which the system has worked so far. Considerable facilities have been created in the institutions over the last number of years and even on the basis of the non-uniform and separate evaluation results themselves, one is rather constrained to find that there is a large wastage in the efforts put in the institutions.

The figures for the out turn at the degree level include those of the IITs also. Taking into account that the wastage at the IITs is very marginal, the wastage naturally is largely accounted for by the other institutions and we may, therefore, say that this would be of the order of about 30 %. Similarly at the diploma level this is as high as 52 %. These figures, if we remember our experience with the system for the last three decades, are not flattering. The Institute of Applied Manpower Research made a study of this problem some time ago. From a survey made by the Institute of the reaction of a few of the students that had undergone these courses, the possible reasons for wastage were stated to be:

a) lack of necessary aptitude for the course among the concerned students;

b) inadequacy of instructional facilities;

c) ineffective teaching, possibly because of the teachers not being trained; and

d) a heavy curriculum.

Valid as these reasons are even today, there may be many other contributory factors also such as:

a) non-selective admission of students to the institutions;

b) changing mix of urban and non-urban background of students without corresponding modifications/ orientation of educational methods contributing to the detriment of the non- urban element;

c) inadequate utilisation of even the existing instruction facilities;

d) in spite of adequate capital investment and hardware provided in the institutions quite often, the lack of appropriate matching provision for adequate departmental operating and training costs;

e) insufficient development of the correct attitudes to the professional education by both the teachers and the students; and

f) external factors, such as lack of motivation because of inadequate or assured employment opportunities at the end of the course.

The intensive study of this problem of wastage is very necessary. This is needed on both academic and planning considerations. Any effort for improvement of existing courses, introduction of new courses, diversification of programmes etc. would be helped a great deal by such feedback information as would be available from such a study. From the planning point of view, any effort to reduce wastage would contribute to the efficiency of the system as such and thus provide for out-turn of additional manpower that may be required without further inputs.

Any efforts at improvement of the system have naturally to take into account the various elements which contribute to its weaknesses as mentioned above. Under the " Quality Improvement Programmes " some steps have been taken to tone up that aspect of the system which concerns the teaching-learning process. Apart from these efforts, which, of course, require to be strengthened to a very great extent, there are other steps which might enhance the effectiveness of the system. Some of these are enumerated below :

(a) Special remedial courses for non-urban/non-elite students It would appear that the courses at present offered, based as they are on urban aptitudes, situations and characteristics, tend to cater to the needs of the elitist group. A majority of the students are from the non-urban sectors and from the institutions in the mofussil/interior areas. The background of the students also is not uniform. in that many of the students may be first or second generation learners. Because of the lack of communication facilities on the same basis as his urban counterpart, such a student would require to be given special orientation/remedial course to be brought on par with the other students. Not only that, even the programmes sometimes have to be appropriately changed to suit his non-urban experience and background.

(b) Multiple entry and flexibility. At present the attitude and aptitude of the students who take these professional courses have no obvious relationship with the professional courses offered to them. Quite often both because of the lack of aptitude, or absence of developing the correct attitude, or because of various other factors such as the duration of the course, the sudden change the student has to undergo in the professional courses as compared to his earlier academic experience, etc., have an adverse effect on his performance. Again for reasons beyond one's control or because of economic and social background etc., the student might have taken up a different course and might like to opt for a professional course at a later stage.

Even within the professional courses, the student might like to change either the branch or particular study which he has chosen earlier, or the orientation of this particular course. Occasionally the possibility of the student having to migrate from one place to another within the country itself also exists. The present system is rather a straight jacket one, with more or less a single entry point and perhaps a rigid course structure. To allow for different types of contingencies, It is necessary to think in terms of multiple entry points (depending upon the earlier academic/field experience) as well as of flexibility of the course structure and organisation.

It is necessary to have a good look at the courses being offered now not merely for the organisational purposes of "graded" facilities. Mere accumulation of information is not knowledge, and complete knowledge by itself does not give the necessary wisdom. The purpose of education is not to produce " educated " individual at one stretch by putting all information and knowledge into course at one time, but, on the other hand, it is to take the individual to progressive stages where he would be in a position to acquire what further information and knowledge he wants for his future activities.

If we accept this philosophy, it is to be conceded that what is important is not to " load " the curriculum but to arrange it in such a way that different requirements and needs of the individual's calling are provided in the process of life-long education. The credit system no doubt can go quite some way in this regard. But a deliberate attempt is to be made to recognise the fact that many of those who pursue these courses of studies will remain as technologists whereas quite a few of them might end up as managers. Further even a technologist has to have sufficient insight into the marginal areas of the allied fields, if not in-depth study in that field itself.

The course content therefore should be so modified as to allow for the technologist to have an overall view in addition to this core discipline, e.g., the professional may have to have managerial training in addition to his professional calling. The education in our institution campuses should break away from the rigid stand of a unidisciplinary approach and a fixed framework but cater to a larger interest to acquaint and give an insight in various fields of expertise of which the institutional faculty and facilities are capable of, by offering on a massive scale refresher courses, study programmes, etc.

Attempts should also be made even in the undergraduate programme to provide for an intensive managerial training for those who desire it within the course frame work apart from those who want to pursue the technological programme. Complementary courses might also be provided for the technologist to acquaint himself with the necessary management techniques and practices, and vice versa.

The infrastructure that has been built up appears to be quite adequate to meet the major requirements of the system for most of the efforts mentioned above. However, with the changing technology and development there may be many areas where specialised personnel are required. A cluster of courses might be required, organisation of diversification on a large scale and occasionally new courses also might be called for. This has to be looked into by appropriate agencies taking care at the same time to see that the fresh inputs for any such effort would be marginal and capable of diversion, whenever required. This is easily said than achieved in practice, but nonetheless the issues are important to be considered.

The facilities available at various levels right from the craftsman to the post-graduate level are adequate and any further expansion of these facilities has to be gone into only after a deep study and with caution. The ratio between the graduate, technician and craftsmen in some of the more industrialised economies is of the orders of 1:3:5; facilities for education being also provided for in that order. With us, the facilities provided at the graduate and technician level are in the ratio of 1:2, but in the output the ratio comes down to about 1:1.

Organisation of any new course/diversification at one or the other levels has to take into consideration a systematic study of the manpower requirement and utilisation, linked with the occupational structure of the various employing sectors. It is, therefore, necessary to keep this in mind while organising any new course/ diversification at any level right from the craftsmen to the post-graduate so that the entire spectrum of activities in the employing fields are kept in mind. This is not to forget the needs of the research and development activities where academic considerations might point to growth potential at a particular level.

While there is no doubt that certain segments of the Technical Education system have built up strong potential (IITs, University Departments, some of the State Colleges, for example), there are others which are rather weak. It is here that practicable and effective system of cooperation programmes between institutions of different types at different levels are to be organised. Desirable are the programmes of exchange of teachers on short term and long-term, on a massive scale planned in relation to specific levels and goals of development, providing opportunities and appropriate programmes for making available at specific and for known periods the facilities available at the better institutions for the use of the staff of the not-so-well-off institutions, organising of special programmes of refresher courses, extension lectures, etc. by the faculty of the better institutions at the other institutions etc.

Efforts at curriculum development, faculty development etc., though now well organised and recognised, have yet to be gone through on a much larger scale and in a more purposeful way. Preparation of manuals for lectures, workshop practice etc., production of text-books, preparation of teaching aids etc. also have to be undertaken by all the institutions by pooling the resources that are available.

For the improvement and further development of the system it is necessary that there is interaction between technical institutions and industry and other field organisations. There has been an awareness of the need for such interaction: creation of agencies such as Industrial Liaison Boards in the States, Co-option of Industrial representatives on the various academic bodies such as the Boards of Management, Boards of Studies etc., and the system of Visiting Professorship/guest lectures etc. has helped to an extent in breaking this ground. But much more remains to be done in this direction. This initiative so far has been with the technical education system with the industry and field organisations, unfortunately, not always showing more than lukewarm interest.

This attitude had radically to be changed in that both technical institutions, who produce manpower for the industry and the field organisations, and also the latter themselves are partners in the same enterprise of developing the economy; and it is high time that this responsibility, is duly realised by setting up this interaction. The employing sector should go all out to associate and involve itself in all matters and at all levels of technical education, planning and implementation. On the other hand, the technical education system should make this possible by appropriate incentives and safeguards for such involvement by personnel from the industry and employing organisations.

A stage has been reached where purely academic consideration in a system of professional education should not be the criteria in determining about the suitability of personnel for technical education. Sufficient credit should be given by the educational authorities for giving appropriate recognition for field expertise- while considering the faculty requirements. Schemes such as adoption of institutions by industry etc., which have been initiated, should be encouraged totally by the industry.

Production of textbooks, other teaching material and teaching aids which have been started now on a small measure have to be considerably stepped up. Manuals for better utilisation of the laboratory and workshop equipment, use of the library as a resource centre both by the teachers and the students have to be encouraged. In all these attempts of preparation of teachers and students materials, emphasis also has to lay on the possible slower comprehension of the non-urban student to the methods employed in the urban situation.

Because of the lack of sufficient 'training' places in industry and field organisations, the provision of training under the Apprenticeship Training Programme has been after the institutional course. For a more effective and coordinated approach, it is necessary to think in terms of integrating the practical/industrial training with the institutional course itself, at appropriate stages of the course. This will lead not only to better supervision but also better comprehension of the field precepts and practices by the student.

## Resource Bank

In terms of the magnitude of human resources and expertise available and of physical facilities created over the last three decades, the system of technical education has become a formidable reservoir of technical expertise, which, perhaps, no other sphere of the economy has developed in such a concentrated manner. What is, therefore, required is to utilise this bank of expertise for the improvement of the system itself as also for the improvement of other elements of the economy. As pointed out, the potential for technical education system both in terms of human and physical resources are so large that it is worthwhile for us to now think from the national stand-point to have a pooled bank for technical expertise and aid, both for domestic or 'external' purpose.

A well organised and processed pool of such resources would be of great advantage for any need in any sector of the economy of the country including the technical education system itself for delivering many of the responsibilities for which now outside help is sought. Indigenous expertise has been sufficiently appreciated and, perhaps, in most of the other countries, we might not have anything better or even as good as what we have among the professionals in the country.

## Community Development

In addition to his own field of specialisation and the group in which he works, the professional has also to discharge his responsibilities satisfactorily both to himself and others in the community. It is necessary, therefore that the professional instead of being in isolation as an individual under training, has also an in built training/education in the environmental aspects so that he will be able to appreciate when he later enters the profession of the various aspects that come to play on his role as a professional in the community. Even as a professional he is not to be considered as if he is in his ivory-tower.

It is necessary that the institutions also are considered as part of the total community activities. While considering the totality of his activity, it becomes imperative that the courses offered at institutions relate to the various demands of the neighbourhood in particular and the community in general, both at present and in the foreseeable future. The education which is offered in the institutions should be of relevance to the various problems that are posed by the society. It is not correct that in their attempts to attain excellence or even the highest standards that the immediate need of the society are forgotten.

The various sector such as rural development including food and agriculture, energy, natural resources (water, mineral oils, forests, etc., both renewable and non-renewable), transport and communications all require immediate attention from the institutions and the courses offered therein. Here it should be recognised that this sort of platitudinous statement is easily made than could be practicable. In our current system of technical education, the main elements of human resources, i.e., the faculty expertise and the student power, if these are to be utilised for the benefit and advantage of the community in the specific sectors mentioned above, a great deal of attention is to be paid as to what exact role these elements have to play in the total set up, as otherwise the danger of the institutions degenerating into more social service organisations, forgetting their real objective of technical education and training is always present.

The academic curriculum for the students should be so organised as to give appropriate credits for practical projects/ service to be made by the students as part of their curricular programme in the investigations taken up by the faculty in the above sectors. Without dilution of he vigorous and curricular content and bringing to bear upon it professional requirements, the possibilities of dovetailing the investigations in the programmes in institutions has to be worked out carefully.

Similarly, the investigations carried out with the existence of the students should be amenable to proper supervisions, scrutiny and appropriate assessment by the faculty who in turn will carry it on further for the benefit of the community without sacrificing the permanent interest of either the institution or the community into which they are looking for the time being. This again underlines the factor that any attempts to take all social projects naturally will have to consider projects of long-term and permanent benefits instead of issues of local popularity or short-term propaganda. This sort of interaction with the problem of the society would help the institution- faculty/the individual students to grow both professionally as also in relevant fields.

## Financial Issues in Technical Education

*Increasing costs*: This brings us to the issue of financing of the technical education system as such. By and large, the efforts at building up and development of the system has so far been under official auspices - either Central and/or States. However, looking into the enormous costs involved, the maintenance of these courses/institutions and the increasing prices around of men and material, it would not be difficult to envisage a situation where let alone the sponsored agencies, but even the Government agencies, would find it difficult to adequately meet the rising cost of technical education. This is a matter of serious concern and has to be faced squarely before it is too late when this system which has been built with so much of care might crumble because of lack of adequate attention.

*Resource Generation by Technical Institutions*: It is true that considerable efforts have to be made by the institutions them- selves for augmenting their resources, by way of various measures for resource generation such as consultancy practice, servicing and testing, production, etc. In connection with the involvement of the system in community services, here again one should not lose sight of the primary objective of the system as such. Any attempt at raising the resources should have only a secondary role that too complimentary to the academic culture of the system and not for its own sake.

If this obvious principle is accepted then the limitations on the institutions raising their own resources will become evident. So, we are left with the major issue again of the provision of adequate funds for the technical education system. It is here, perhaps, one should consider the ways and means by which large users of the products of the system also share the responsibility adequately for the cost of production. There have been suggestions over the years in this direction for motivation by way of incentives, or raising of resources by levying a technical education cess on the users etc. Certain incentives, of course, have been offered by giving to an extent exemption for industry in Income Tax, towards contribution to educational programmes and for a cess in the research and development establishment for R & D purposes.

But, however, this has not resulted in a large shift and on the whole most of the burden has been solely on that of the Government. This has been because technical education has been considered as part of social service and governmental responsibility for the social welfare programmes has had to take care of such programmes. It is now necessary for us to have a detailed and fresh look at this issue.

## Qualification Assessment of Technical Education

The Board of Assessment of Qualifications of the Government of India, which also deals with professional qualifications and equivalence of various awards has a limited view of assessment for a specific purpose, i.e., for governmental employment. Further, as it is practiced, the work of the Assessment Board is a sort of one time evaluation based on a minimum requirement. For a healthy and effective growth, what is required is a sort of continuous and objective assessment aiming at higher and still higher standards.

Even though many agencies, particularly, statutory agencies are involved and any such attempt may not be looked upon with unmixed favour, the point to be remembered is that we should without further delay, strengthen our system, by identifying the weaknesses and strength of a particular sector/course/institutions so that there is adequate motivation and direction for further improvement. This comprehensive purpose of assessment, not limited for any objective of recruitment by official agencies only, will act as a spur when such evaluation and assessment is done periodically. This agency for accreditation and evaluation of standards should be a national agency, with perhaps, regional and sectoral wings, as may be required.

Professional organisations and persons of standing in the profession and representatives of accredited user agencies should be intimately involved in the work of an agency. A system of frequent and periodical evaluation with provision for a graded scale of attainment of individual courses/departments should be the objective. Such an agency might work under the auspices of the Ministry of Education but not as a part of it; it should be an autonomous Organisation so that it would be free to draw upon expertise wherever available.

# 2

# Curriculum Methods and Instructional Strategies of Professional Education

On the threshold of the 21st century, schooling systems worldwide are in a flux. They are grappling with the mandate of training it's future generation to function in a knowledge economy. This is a tremendous challenge as the teachers from this generation have themselves been a product of schooling aimed at mass producing input for an industrial society. The new competencies identified by the OECD point to a glaring gap between the demands of society and the capacity of teachers to answer to it.

Teacher professional development had incredibly tight spaces to navigate. Few teachers embody new competencies. Yet the preparation and capacity building of teachers is the keystone of national policy being operationalised into practice.

In India, the constitution guarantees 8 years of compulsory schooling. Education has always been based on a national curriculum framework but programmes of study have been localised at the state boards of education level. Most of the practice emanating from the programmes of study is driven by the high-stakes public exams to be taken at the end of grade 10 and grade 12. The constitution under the 86th amendment of December 2002 has made elementary education(ages 6-14) a fundamental right. Curriculum discourse has undergone regular revisions in the five decades since independence but the practice of it is still rooted in the British legacy. Curriculum frameworks now emphasise competencies and process over skills and content. It openly acknowledges the gap between the new competencies demanded in the curriculum and the preparation of the teachers to address it. Different organisational responses to in-service teacher professional development expiains as the following:

*Government Education Departments*: Education has been on the concurrent list (both state and center are responsible for it) for almost two decades now. There is a national council(NCERT) responsible for structuring and arranging in-service teacher training. In 1993, an Act of Parliament established a National Council of Teacher Education (NCTE) as statutory body to provide oversight for in-service development.

*District Institutes of Education and Training (DIETs) and Colleges of Education*: While these are very active at the pre-service level(over 75% of the teaching force is formally trained) they play a minimal role in in-service teacher training. While some of them conduct short-term "refresher" courses for teachers, the schools are generally not supportive of teachers attending these courses during the school year. The teachers are required to do this on their own time. It is not part of their job time.

*Educational Societies*: Educational Societies run more than one school. These are private schools but receive grant-in-aid for their students. (The system is similar to vouchers and the schools have no geographical relation to where the students reside). These societies organise summer workshops for their teachers

*Voluntary Agencies*: In India there are a large number of voluntarily agencies that work for the betterment of school education. These agencies arrange training courses for practicing teachers sometimes with the help of education department, sometimes without their help. The work of these agencies usually remains limited to a certain region, and they focus on local specific problems. Since the members of voluntary agencies work as resource persons without any remuneration and teachers attend these courses on their own without demanding any conveyance charges, such course are often cost effective.

Teachers are typically not supported if they do take the initiative to participate in these programmes (in terms of remuneration, substitute teachers being arranged to take their classes, etc.). On the contrary, many schools actually discourage teachers from taking time off for these programmes. Because there are no arrangements available for teacher substitution, the burden of "keeping the children busy" simply falls on some other teacher's shoulders. Teachers who do take part in in-service programmes carry back a "certificate of participation" but little more than that. Some schools may give an extra increment in salary at the end of the year, based on such certificates. No contact is maintained between the teachers and the resource providers following completion of the workshop or programme, i.e., there is little by way of follow-up action. In-service teacher training is largely an unorganised effort.

## National Council of Teacher Education (NCTE)

The broad mandate given to the NCTE is to achieve planned and co-ordinated development of the teacher education system throughout the country, the regulation and proper maintenance of norms and standards in the teacher education system and for matters connected therewith. The responsibility of regulating quality of teacher education through norms and standards came to the NCTE when teacher education system had already seen its mushroom growth.

Teacher education underwent expansion in different parts of the country that too in heterogeneous conditions and was even used by some institutions as a money spinner programmeme, as surplus of income over expenses could be ensured by running it in a diluted form. Role of NCTE was generally perceived as a threat, as it involved conflict of interests, and was opposed as it curbed unfettered freedom for exploiting teacher education for commercial purposes. By developing resource materials in print and electronic forms and distributing them to teacher education institutions NCTE has been playing a catalytic role in the process of change of teacher education and for making it relevant to the context of learning today. It is hoped that teacher educators will pick up the new ideas and that they will be able to reorient teacher education programmemes for giving to the school system such teachers as can competently take care of education of children for the 21st century.

## A Case Study of Role of Voluntary Agencies - Eklavya

About three decades ago, a group of young science graduates started a programme to improve the teaching of science in rural areas in the Hoshangabad district of Madhya Pradesh, a state in central India. Eventually calling themselves Ekalavya, the name of a mythological lower caste archery expert, the group emphasised the importance of making science interesting and relevant to rural children. In response to this initiative, the state government at that time allowed them to try out their curriculum at government schools. Thus emerged the Hoshangabad Science Teaching Programme (HSTP). It is based on an inquiry-oriented, experiment-based and environment-related child-friendly pedagogy. The programme covers about 1,000 schools with around 2,500 science teachers and covers over 100,000 children every year.

The report submitted by the Evaluation Committee constituted by the Department of Education, Ministry of Human Resource Development, Govt. of India, after 20 years of it's operation in 1991, to evaluate the implementation of Hoshangabad Science Teaching Programme (HSTP) calls out as exemplary the teacher training process. Recognising that teachers will need scaffolding to implement a curriculum alien to their ingrained way of thinking HSTP put in place a programme of continuous teacher professional development. About 2000 teachers have been given an intensive training. Out of these a large group of Resource Persons have emerged, who in turn have been training other teachers. Periodical refresher courses and more important, a constant interaction with scientists, educationists, trainers, resource persons and fellow-teachers is a major component of the programme.

The concept of "Sangam Kendra", monthly meetings is providing the much needed strength to the programme. The long standing success of this programme has been it's ability to empower regular science teachers with the inspiration to become one with the new pedagogical style. This response is a case study of a voluntary agency working with the local people and the government to set up an institutional framework for an ongoing teacher education programme. The end of this story about HSTP however serves to underline the fact that curriculum is the most political of all aspects of education. In this case, the state government succeeded in shutting down this programme in 2003 after much lobbying by a local politician.

In spite of extensive institutional success and grass roots excitement, the political elite of that regime felt that the social science curriculum(which was a parallel programme of HSTP) was based on a political ideology and that it was being used as a vehicle for political change. While political activism was not the aim of HSTP socio-political awareness was one of the framings used to design the curriculum and the instructional package. Ironically, the programme was closed down under a state government whose philosophy is based not on fundamentalist Hindu principles but on secular ones.

India has made great strides in education. She has used the bi-lingual legacy of the British rule to great advantage when positioning herself as a supplier of a technical and scientific workforce. Why is the larger picture still so dismal? The sheer size of the population makes any reform effort at the national level a near impossible dream. India will benefit from decentralising educational policy making if it adopts national guidelines and delegates the operationalisation of this agenda to the local decision making bodies. The discourse being publicly disseminated resonates with international demands and definitions of new competencies.

In India on the other hand, access for the entire population is still an issue but the country seems to be concerned on both things, providing access to all but providing quality to those that are part of it. In India the cultural diversity within the country has occasioned the government to address other issues like local languages and they have both solved the problem in diverse ways. Mexico promotes bilingual education for indigenous communities enabling first the use of the native language and as second language Spanish.

India in particular mentions that it has an international competitive edge provided by the content heavy curriculum and is unwilling to sacrifice that at the altar of the process heavy curriculum.

– *Distance Education*: In India, there are some distance education programmes. Even though the intent of the government appears to be to make ongoing professional development more accessible, enrollment figures indicate otherwise.

- *Front and center on national agenda*: India openly acknowledge the gap between the official dialog about the curriculum and the competencies of the teachers to achieve it. India keen to provide the necessary strategies to breach it.
- *Pre-service teacher preparation*: This is mandatory in India and over 90% of all teachers undergo some level of professional training.
- *Incentives*: In India there is no mandated incentive or scheme of followup.
- *Institutional framework*: India mandates 20 days/year as reserved for ongoing training but has not organised framework to deliver the courses.
- *Professional Status*: India aware of the need to improve the status of teachers professionally.

One official evaluation by the Indian government openly laments at the lack of research in an innovative curriculum reform project.

## Information Infrastructure for Professional

Information Technology (IT) applications have brought tremendous change in the total scenario of information storage, access and dissemination. Advancement of telecommunication and networking technologies have facilitated faster methods of information access and delivery. The developments of Internet and the World Wide Wave has made a tremendous impact in the society as a whole, shrinking the world into a global village.

In this changing scenario the information professionals play a vital role. Manpower constitutes the most important component of the National Information Infrastructure, which needs to be well planned for the development of the country as such. IT revolution has already taken its root in

India creating a heavy demand for the information professionals in the country.

With information and communication technologies becoming useful in all areas of human activity, the information handling and retrieval skills are becoming more desirable across the whole spectrum of workforce. However, in the present set up, the LIS courses offered by the universities and other institutions are not properly geared for the emerging market. It has, therefore, become imperative to reassess the market for the information professionals and device strategies to meet the current need.

The information technology revolution started in India in the 1980s when microcomputers were introduced for railway reservation and office automation. Gradually technologies such as telefacsimile, teletext, videotext, satellite television etc. were introduced. During the Seventh Five Year Plan (1987-1992) introduction of technologies viz. Digital switching systems, digital microwave, use of optical fibre for long distance transmission, multi-access rural radio system in rural networks were the major accomplishments.

In the Eighth Five Year Plan (1992-1997) many value added services such as cellular mobile services, voice and electronic mail services, audio and video conferencing services and radio paging services were started. In the networking frontier, several important initiatives were made during the Seventh Five-Year Plan. Data networks such as NICNET (for government departments), and INDONET (for public and commercial use) became operational.

Specialised networks such as INFLIBNET (for all the university and specialised research and development institution libraries), DESINET (for Defence Science laboratories), SIRNET (for laboratories of the Council for Scientific and Industrial Research) were conceived. Under the ERNET project, scientific and industrial institutions were connected through e-mail. Several metropolitan library networks viz., DELNET, CALIBNET, MALIBNET, BONET etc. were also initiated during the seventh and the eighth plan periods.

Since 1990s, India has witnessed significant economic reforms. There has been paradigm shift in its national development strategies, moving from protectionism, self-reliance and central planning to policies emphasising liberalisation, global integration and market driven growth. Restructuring initiatives in telecommunications, informatics and broadcasting are also part of these socio-economic reforms.

The recent policy initiatives are directed towards developing the country's National Information Infrastructure. In the recent years there has been interesting developments in the telecom and broadcasting sectors. As per the National Telecom Policy, all of India's 600,000 villages are expected to be provided with telephone exchanges by the year 1997. From the current level of 12 million lines, over 30 million telephone lines are expected by the year 2000. The cellular services are currently available in major cities which is to be extended to the other cities by the end of this year.

Around 2.5 million cellular phones are expected by the year 2000. Major developments were also witnessed in the broadcasting and satellite communication sector. Until the early 1990s broadcasting was a state monopoly in India. With the Supreme Court ruling in February 1995, airwaves were declared public allowing private companies to broadcast radio and television signals either through terrestrial means or through satellites. As a result there has been a boom both in the number of viewership and the number of broadcasters.

It is expected that by the year 2000 there will be around hundred television channels. In the networking front, Internet is being adopted in a big way throughout the country. Though currently there are around 16,000 Net users, the number is quite insignificant as compared to the population of around 950 million. However, by the end of this year the total number of connectivity is expected to be around 100,000. It is expected that apart from the commercial users, the educational institutions, universities, and government organisations will come forward to rapidly expand and fully exploit the usage of the Internet. All these developments have direct implication for the information professionals, and they need to be geared up for the current market requirement.

## Status of the Information Profession

After the independence in 1947, LIS schools in India proliferated at a fast pace. The LIS courses are being conducted at various levels in India. Currently there are more than ninety universities and institutions offering BLIS, fifty seven offering MLIS and about thirty nine universities conducting Ph.D. programmes. The certificate and diploma level courses are being conducted by the library associations, polytechnics etc. Apart from these conventional courses, there are associateship courses in Information Science and in Documentation and Information offered by Indian National Scientific Documentation Centre (INSDOC), New Delhi and Documentation Research and Training Centre (DRTC), Bangalore.

Some of the institutions viz., INSDOC, DRTC, NISSAT(National Information System for Science and Technology ) and the library associations also offer short term Continuing Professional Education programmes from time to time. Most of the LIS schools in India follow traditional curriculum, which are inadequate to meet the demand of the emerging market. This calls for reassessment of strategies for developing competent manpower. The existing curriculum of most of the universities are based on the recommendation of the Ranganathan Committee and the Committee set up by the University Grants Commission (UGC) in 1978.

The recommendations made by these committees where mainly for the Bachelors level courses which are quite outdated and irrelevant in the present day context. In order to restructure the curriculum and bring about a uniform national pattern of LIS education in India, the University Grants Commission (UGC) appointed the Curriculum Development Committee(CDC) in 1990. The Report brought out by the CDC was however found to be unsatisfactory and was not adopted by most of the universities. In view of the latest developments in the information technology and rising demand for the information professionals, there is an urgent need to develop strategies conducive for the National Information Infrastructure.

## Training Needs of Information Professionals

How to generate appropriate manpower for the National Information Infrastructure is the major issue confronting the information profession today. As a result of wide range application of information and communication technologies, the nature of information work has undergone a wide change over the last two decades. In the context of the emerging Information Society, information organisation, dissemination and management is getting more emphasis.

The developments in the Internet, multimedia technology, web etc., have changed the whole scenario of information management. There is a distinct change in the role of the information professionals as compared to the traditional roles and responsibilities. Adoption of wide range of information technologies for information related work calls for redefinition of services, roles and responsibilities of the information professionals. For providing effective services, the modern information professionals need to acquire knowledge and skills of different professions viz. computer and software specialist, database managers, publishers, journalist and media specialists etc.

There is a rising demand for a new kind of information workers accomplished with the skills of various professions. The information professionals need to be properly trained in information technology applications and information handling procedures to adapt themselves to the changed environment. Keeping in view the changes taking place in the society, there is a strong need to develop adequate number of trained information professionals with specialised skills for the emerging market.

With information work becoming multifunctional in nature, it has become essential to incorporate changes in the curriculum by adopting multi-disciplinary approach. The greatest challenge for the professional courses is to bring together the skills of the librarians, computer scientists, and subject specialists. There is also an urgent need to attract more number of persons to the profession. Unless immediate steps are taken to develop adequate number of modern information professionals, chances are there that persons from the other professions will have an upper hand in the information related work and the LIS professionals will be left with the traditional roles of managing libraries.

This will restrict the development of the profession and create a glut in the market for the LIS professionals. Thus, redesigning and restructuring the curriculum for the LIS courses, has become the foremost task of the profession and special attention is needed in this direction. Information technology revolution has already taken its root in India and this has profound implication for the information professionals. Manpower constitutes the most important component of any infrastructure. Therefore for developing National Information Infrastructure, it is important to look into the education and the training needs of the information professionals.

The foremost task of the LIS schools should be to develop professionals specialising in handling of the new information technology. Special emphasis should be given to impart skills and training in handling of latest technological innovations. The curriculum should be flexible enough to adopt changes as and when required. The curriculum should try to integrate the information technology aspects with the general curriculum. Traditional skills of librarianship in information handling is important and hence it should not be sidelined. The traditional skills of information processing, retrieval and dissemination are to be reoriented with the new information technology to suit the present day situation. The curriculum should therefore incorporate the traditional skills with new approach, merging the content with the new information technology.

In a fast changing society, it may not be possible for any generalistic curriculum to take care of all the aspects of information work. It is therefore imperative to develop curriculum at different levels. The courses should be developed in three levels: generic, specialised and advanced levels. The generic courses should provide knowledge and experience in information processing, resources and services. The specialised courses should provide extensive experience and skills in the new information technology at technical and operational level.

The advanced level courses should be mainly for developing professional expertetise. These courses should be providing high level of skills in handling different information technologies. While restructuring the curriculum to suit the current needs of information infrastructure, special attention is also required to develop sufficient number of qualified faculty. Well-trained faculty is the most crucial requirement for implementing changes in the curriculum.

It is therefore important to reorient and reeducate the faculty from time to time to keep them abreast of the latest developments in the profession. Moreover, the multidisciplinary approach of the curriculum will require cooperation from other disciplines. The faculty could comprise of two categories: the generic and the specialist. While the generic faculty would be providing knowledge and training in information handling procedures, the specialist would impart skills and training in handling of various information and communication technologies, management techniques etc.

The strategies mentioned above could be only fruitful if proper infrastructural facilities are available with the institutions imparting education and training to the information professionals. It is therefore essential for the institutions to have adequate infrastructure in terms of computer and communication technologies- both hardware and software, sufficient access to multimedia learning resources, and well trained staff to handle and maintain the resources.

# 3

# Universalisation of Secondary Education

All education is necessarily good, both for the individual and for society, and that it will necessarily lead to progress, can be as harmful as it is misplaced. Quantitatively, education can be organised to promote social justice or to retard it. History shows numerous instances where small social groups and elites have used education as a prerogative of their rule and as a tool for maintaining their hegemony and perpetuating the values upon which it has rested. On the other hand, there are cases in which a social and cultural revolution has been brought about in a system where equality of educational opportunity is provided and education is deliberately used to develop more and more potential talent and to harness it to the solution of national problems. The same is even more true of the quality of education.

Universal secondary education is no more a luxury but a pre-condition for equitable social development, widening participation in India's democratic functioning, building up of an enlightened secular republic, and be globally competitive. The latest figures of 'Drop Out' rates reveal that almost half of the child population enrolled in schools does not complete even eight years of elementary education. This is despite the internationally funded DPEP from 1993-

94 onwards and now almost three years of Sarva Shiksha Abhiyan (SSA).

UNESCO's Global Monitoring Report of 2002 has made detailed projections and concluded that India is unlikely to achieve UEE even by 2015! In this sense, India is categorised along with Pakistan, Nepal and some of the middle east and sub-Saharan countries; some of the South Asian neighbouring countries like Sri Lanka and Bangladesh have done better than India. These warnings are important since the ambition of the Indian State is to emerge as a developed nation by 2020. A successful programme of Universal Elementary Education is the precondition for taking the first reliable step towards Universal Secondary Education.

The success of UEE will lie in objectively reviewing the very premises on which the present policies and programmes are founded and reconstructing the policies on the basis of the outcome of such a review. Universal Secondary Education cannot be merely quantitative expansion or an illuminated carbon copy of what exists today. The very concept of secondary education needs to be reconstructed in the context of today and tomorrow.

Following four guiding principles may act as the pillars on which the edifice of Universal Secondary Education should be built in the years to come:

*Universal Access*: Access is to be envisaged in physical, social, cultural and economic terms - all interwoven in a common concept. This calls for a redefinition of some of the basic features of the Indian school. For instance, it is not sufficient to provide physical access to an orthopaedically disabled child. It is equally critical that the disability of such a child is not seen in medical terms alone. The moment a barrier-free physical access is provided, this child's disability disappears and she becomes as capable as the rest of her peers. In this sense, the disability is a social construct and the matter does not end by solving the problem at the physical level alone but demands a change in the mindsets of her classmates, teachers and the curriculum planners or textbook writers.

Similarly, in the case of a dalit child, access is as much a cultural question as it is one of a school being available in the neighbourhood. There are poignant accounts of how alienating and humiliating school experience can be for children of the deprived sections of society. This kind of alienation is equally visible in gender discrimination as it operates as a 'hidden curriculum' all the time as an extension of patriarchy embedded in society. In these circumstances, children don't just 'drop out' voluntarily, but either they are 'pushed out' or even 'walk out' in protest. It is only when the school is able to create a new cultural ambience and a childfriendly curriculum that universal access would begin to mean more than just concrete, black boards or even computers.

*Equality and Social Justice*: These two fundamental principles as enshrined in the Constitution imply equality and social justice towards secondary education, inside secondary education and through secondary education. It is only when the school curriculum empowers the child adequately to initially understand, then question and finally deal with that inequality and injustice, the child would be in a position to continue to seek equality and social justice in her life after the school. This is not all. Following are six dimensions of equality and social justice for which the school system will have to strive for viz.

a) gender;

b) economic disparity;

c) social i.e. SCs/STs;

d) Cultural (including the issues of religious and linguistic diversity);

e) disability (both physical and mental), and

f) rural-urban.

All these dimensions need to be reflected with sensitivity in the curriculum such that the self-esteem of each child is built up. This is necessary for ensuring that all children are able to complete their secondary education. The issue has a structural dimension too. Almost 25% of the secondary schools today are private unaided schools whose clientele comes only from the privileged sections of society. This means that the children studying in such schools are deprived of the experience of knowing children of different social classes and diverse cultural backgrounds.

It is inconceivable that such schools can inculcate a sense of equality or social justice among their students or even build up an appreciation of the composite culture and plural character of India. This anomaly can be taken care of only by including the private unaided schools in a Common School System, as recommended by the Education Commission (1964-66).

*Relevance and Development*: No education today can be accepted as being relevant unless it

a) helps in unfolding the full potential of the child; and

b) plays the role of linking the development of the child with the society and its political, productive and socio-cultural dimensions.

A substantial proportion of parents send their children to schools with expectation that education will enable their children to face the 'world of work' with confidence and carve out a meaningful livelihood for themselves. For this purpose, it is essential that learning emerges from the child's social ethos and her productive experience, and at the same time ensures that the child will have access to global knowledge and challenges.

*Structural and Curricular Aspects*: Curricular reforms cannot be delinked from structural reforms. There is a consensus today throughout the country with respect to the 10+2 pattern of school education, as recommended by the

Education Commission (1964-66). The Education Commission had also advocated that a minimum of 10 years of common curriculum is required for building citizenship in a democracy and for linking the 'world of knowledge' with the 'world of work'. In this concept, diversified courses will be introduced only at the +2 stage. These recommendations related to curriculum could be implemented by all States/ UTs only because the Central Government enabled a nation-wide switchover to the 10+2 pattern.

In contrast, the policy on vocational education of "diverting" at least 25% of the children enrolled at the + 2 stage to the vocational stream by the year 2000 has not found favour with students. According to the Ministry's Annual Reports, less than 5% of the enrolment at the + 2 stage in the year 2003 was in vocational stream. One can infer that the children refused to be "diverted" and preferred the academic stream. The issue has been recently addressed by the National Focus Group on 'Work and Education', as constituted by NCERT, as part of the exercise of reviewing and revising the curriculum framework.

The above report recommends a two-pronged strategy with radical structural and curricular implications for the entire school education, including secondary education, viz.

a) Productive work must be introduced in the curriculum as a pedagogic medium for acquisition of knowledge, building values and skill formation from pre-primary stage to the + 2 stage;

b) A nation-vide programme of Vocational Education and Training (VET) must be built up in mission mode and be structurally and administratively placed outside the school system incorporating modular courses with lateral and vertical linkages.

As long as the proposed twopronged strategy of simultaneous structural and curricular reforms is not institutionaliased, it is inconceivable that the "world of work" can be meaningfully integrated with the "world of knowledge" and vocational education can become a significant and effective programme. The four guiding principles, namely universal access, equality and social justice, relevance and development, and structural and curricular aspects as guiding principles together imply a paradigm shift necessary for moving towards the goal of Universalisation of Secondary Education. This shift is expected to simultaneously impact at the level of access, socio-cultural character, developmental objectives and structural-cum-curricular provisions of secondary education - all at the same time and throughout the nation.

## Nature of Secondary Education

It is time that we recognise the rising levels of democratic consciousness and social aspirations among the young people in the age group of 14-18 years, particularly from the deprived sections of society including girls and the disabled, for a greater share in nation's political, social and techno-economic life. This pressure is expected to take a quantum jump consequent upon the anticipated progress in the UEE by 2010. In view of this, the Central and the State/ UT governments must jointly initiate planning to implement the agenda of universal and free secondary education in the first phase by the year 2015 and then extend it to senior secondary education in the second phase by the year 2020.

The conventional expectation from secondary/senior secondary education lies in its role in creating the necessary base for generating technical person power, raising the potential of a society in contributing to the growth of knowledge and skills and thereby enhancing the nation's capacity to face the challenge of global competitiveness. That in itself constitutes a significant part of the vision. However, this is not all. The contemporary and additional expectation from secondary education is to build a democratic citizenship that is committed to the Constitutional goal of enabling India to move towards an egalitarian, secular and enlightened society while also being sensitive to India's rich cultural and linguistic diversity and its composite culture. There is yet another dimension.

In order to extend the access of secondary education to the hitherto marginalised sections of society, comprising almost two-thirds of the 14-18 year age group population, and make their participation at this level genuinely inclusive, it would become imperative that the long-overdue changes in the social, cultural and pedagogic character of the secondary/senior secondary school are not delayed any further. Indeed, such changes are expected to benefit even those sections that manage at present to participate in and survive through secondary education, inspite of its exclusionary character. This implies that universalisation of secondary education can not be envisaged merely in terms of quantitative expansion of what we have today.

Universalisation calls for a paradigm shift founded on four guiding principles that involve reconceptualisation of access itself, socio-cultural ambience of the classroom, notion of knowledge, values and skills and the relationship between what is learnt inside the school and what is available outside. Without such a paradigm shift, the goal of Universalisation of Secondary Education is as likely to elude the policy makers as has been the case with the UEE agenda for more than half a century.

Echoing the Indian wisdom, the International Commission on Education for the 21st Century also mentioned human beings live in four planes namely physical, intellectual, mental and spiritual. Accordingly, future citizens of India should be physically strong and sound, intellectually competent, mentally/emotionally matured and intelligent, and spiritually intelligent and enriched to be creative, innovative and exploring. To support education at four planes, the Commission identified four pillars of learning, namely, learning to know, learning to do, learning to live together and learning to be. Physical qualities will include internally sound and disease free long life, physical skills at work and play, etc. reflecting learning to know as well as learning to do.

Intellectual skills should display multiple intelligence at the best of the potentials; and also transcending from lower to higher order cognition nurturing creativity with emphasis on learning to know. Emotional qualities are the emotional intelligence that makes significant contribution to corporate and social life and 'learning to live together'. Spiritual skills would be woven around the concept of 'learning to be', particularly, linking oneself to larger social, national, global and cosmic goals.

Future education, then, would be a holistic responsive education facilitating manifestation of perfection already in man and woman. It also implies the cognitive, emotive and physical attributes of future citizens to be founded on a sound value paradigm. This will require re-conceptualising secondary education and a building a fresh new concept. Emphasis in secondary education has to be shifted from 'mugging up' a few content items for writing examination to school as holistic living experience. This implies a paradigm shift in the conceptualisation of secondary education itself. This would also mean that secondary education cannot be treated only as a production function of the economy, nor can it be justified only on the ground that it contributes to human capital formation and large majority of school graduates will enter the work force. Conceptually, it has to be more inclusive - justifying on the ground that every child has right to exercise her/his full potential and achieve excellence; education has the potentiality and 'state' has the responsibility in facilitating unfolding that potential and achieving the excellence hidden in every individual.

Contemporary secondary education concentrates primarily on learning a few subjects challenging the 'cognitive intelligence', that too largely the lower order cognition. This very approach to secondary education disables a large number of students because students with differential intelligence are unable to cope with the demands of the kind of education offered in secondary education; on the other hand, secondary education do not contribute and nurture the. differential intelligence that children bring with them to the school. For example, a talented sports genius is ridiculed for low scores in mathematics or geography.

The future secondary education must be designed to nurture multiple intelligence like linguistic or verbal intelligence, logical-mathematical intelligence, spatial intelligence, bodily-kinesthetic or sports intelligence, musical intelligence, inter-personal intelligence, intra-personal intelligence and naturalist or environmental intelligence. The Committee does not necessarily propose and recommend adoption or adaptation of Howard Gardener's model of multiple intelligence lock stock and barrel. The primary intention of designing secondary education with a multiple intelligence framework is to ensure that a young person with musical ability can emerge a musician, one with bodily and kinesthetic intelligence is able to emerge as a sportsperson, as much as the person with linguistic intelligence can unfold himself or herself as an orator, a writer, etc.

Equally important is nurturing the logical-mathematical intelligence that can produce a scholar in mathematics and science and other such scholastic subjects. In absence of education designed to facilitate multiple intelligence, children with intelligence other than mathematical-logical intelligence are dubbed as nonintelligent or less intelligent. This not only makes them underachievers but also demolishes their self-concept and self esteem. In essence, for universalisation, secondary education must offer adequate opportunity for exercising all varieties of intelligence and unfolding the full potential in each student.

### *Education for Adolescence*

Secondary education spreads over the ages of 15 and 16, and then to 17 and 18 in the senior secondary grades. These are the years of adolescence, and late adolescence. These are the years of transition; indeed, most crucial years of life. There are steady and fast changes in the body structure transforming to adult form and image of life. At this age, the bodily changes take final shape and stabilise. Established theories of intelligence also indicate that growth of intelligence stabilise at this age, although the new generation brain research indicates that because of continuous reorganisation of brain neurons, intelligence may continue to grow beyond this age.

From the angle of multiple intelligence, this age is the most significant since the potentialities unfold faster and stabilise. The childhood voice cracks and takes the final shape (important for budding musicians); majority of the players show their final promise at this stage, and so on. This is also the stage of emotional transformation and maturity that swings between joy and trauma. Secondary education essentially has to be the education of the adolescence. Experiences in schooling have to be designed to be responsive to the needs of transition and stabilisation.

Since large number of students are likely to transit from education to the world of work, it is also the stage of transition to work. Secondary education must foster skills of transition. Though both boys and girls experience transition, there is a special case for girls and it needs special attention. Because of prejudices, taboos and social stigma, phase of transition for girls is more difficult. Child marriage, still prevalent in many parts of the country is a stumbling block for girls education. Also, it will be necessary to develop a gender friendly curriculum.

In the context of education, 'universal', 'free', and 'compulsory' can be used simultaneously although three have altogether different meanings. There are countries where education is free but not universal, there are others where certain levels of education are universal but not free; there are yet others where education is free and also compulsory. For example, with the amendment of the Constitution, elementary education for the children in the age group 6 to 14 must be universal, free and compulsory.

Education at the preschool level, however, can be universal and free, but not compulsory. Committee is of the view that secondary education should be universal and free but not compulsory. By universal it means, then creating universal access and opportunity for all children to receive secondary education. It is important and meaningful. It is evident from the international experience that secondary education becomes naturally universal once universal elementary education has been achieved. The transition rate from eighth to the ninth grades in India is almost 85 per cent and this transition rate is further improving.

With the universalisation of elementary education through SSA, there will be universal demand for secondary education. What is important is to create access for universal secondary education which need not be free and should not be compulsory. Universal secondary education had to be differentially subsidised, almost total state responsibility for providing secondary education to economically weaker sections of the society, and moderately subsidised for those who can afford.

On age, the Committee recommends universal secondary education by 2015; the projection of enrolment, transition rate indicates full possibility of universal enrolment in secondary education by 2015. By 2020, the target should be universal enrolment, full retention and mastery learning in all kinds of learning tasks by more than 60% learners. Also, by 2020, there will be provision for universal senior secondary education and universal retention. This will be possible because of high transition rate from 10th to 11th standard and high retention rate in the senior secondary grades even now.

Examining the situation prevailing in mid-1960's with respect to curricular structure at the secondary level, the Education Commission (1964-66) recommended its reorganisation in the following words: "The first step in this direction would be the abandoning of the present higher secondary pattern in which specialisation begins in class IX, and the institution of a new higher secondary course beginning in class XI. "While recommending a nation-wide shift to 10+2+3 pattern, the Commission visualised that "the first ten years of schooling.....will provide a course of general education without any specialisation."

The Commission further clarified that "the system of 'streaming' in schools of general education, which now [i.e. in mid-1960s] begins in class IX, should be given up and no attempt at specialisation should be made till after class X." This recommendation for a common curriculum until class X within the 10+2+3 framework was accepted in NPE-1968 and a major programme of shift with additional outlays was undertaken throughout the country. NPE-1986 reiterated this pattern of education as part of the National System of Education. The National Curriculum Framework (1975) proposed a common curriculum for the ten-year school, to be followed by diversification beginning at class XI for the +2 stage. This basic principle is now practiced nation-wide.

The National Curriculum Frameworks prepared successively in 1988, 2000 and 2005 have continued to follow this imperative of NPE-1986. It is in this background that the Committee examined the proposal from certain quarters that diversification should be pre-poned to class IX. The proponents of this view contend that "the most significant reason for mass scale failure in the tenth board examination is the common curriculum and course offerings..... nearly 80 per cent of the candidates who fail in the board examination fail in mathematics, English and science..... besides significant wastage of the educational resources, it affects self-esteem and self-concept of the students."

The solution offered by these proponents to the problem of "mass scale failure in the tenth board examination" and its adverse impact on the "selfesteem" of students consisted in "diversification of students into several streams of education beyond eighth standard" and offering them a "cafeteria approach" from class IX onwards. This view was debated by the Committee at length. In the view of the Committee, however, the root cause of "mass scale failure" is not the common curriculum offered until class X as per NPE-1986. Instead, the cause of the failure lies in the framework in which subject knowledge is conceived, the manner in which knowledge is transacted and the evaluation parameters and the assessment procedures adopted for examining students.

The right to study and succeed in basic mathematics, science, social science and languages, including English, and other mainstream subjects is as much a fundamental right of a child as to have access to and complete secondary/ senior secondary education. Keeping this in mind, the National Curriculum Framework - 2005 has made several radical proposals to revisit the very character of knowledge, shift to a new pedagogic approach and change the entire examination system. Such changes are urgently required in order to make sure that the nation is freed of this phenomenon of "mass scale failure" and widespread but apparent "under-achievement". Without such a paradigm shift, it would not be possible to universalise secondary education either.

We need to be especially concerned about the prevailing practice of not offering science or mathematics at Plus Two stage in many rural schools/ urban slums or to

SCs, STs, girls or the disabled (or not providing science labs at class IX-X level in backward areas), thereby forcing these children to go in for the so-called "softer" options. This practice has a significant negative impact on the aspirations of the masses for upward social mobility for their children.

***Work and Education***

"Based upon the report (April, 2005) of the National Focus Group on Work and Education constituted by NCERT as part of its exercise of revising the existing National Curriculum Framework, the Committee expresses its deep concern with respect to the exclusionary character of education in general and secondary education in particular. This is founded on the artificially instituted dichotomy between work and knowledge (also reflected in the widening gap between school and society). Those who work with their hands and produce significant wealth are denied access to formal education while those who have access to formal education not only denigrate productive manual work but also lack the necessary skills for the same.

The socio-cultural, gender and disabilityrelated dimensions of this dichotomy have serious implications. Such education has come to be embedded in the knowledge system, representing the dominant classes/castes/cultures/ languages with gender in each of these categories. The education system has tended to 'certify' this form of knowledge as being the only 'valid' form. In the process, the knowledge inherent among the vast productive forces along with the related values and skills has been excluded from the school curriculum." "The Committee also takes note of how the pedagogic role of productive work was time and again either marginalised or trivialised in the school curriculum by equating it with either 'work experience' or Socially Useful Productive Work (SUPW). Accordingly, the Committee recommends the following two-fold strategy for a major curricular reform:

- Productive work (and other forms of work as well, including social action and engagement) may be introduced as a pedagogic medium for knowledge acquisition, developing values and multiple-skill formation. A common core curriculum incorporating work-centred pedagogy initially until Class X and, within the foreseeable future, up to Class XII for all children, should be the objective. A set of work-related generic competencies (Basic, Inter-personal and Systemic) may be pursued and also inform the redesigning of evaluation parameters as well as the assessment system, including the public examinations. Generic competencies will include, among others, critical thinking, transfer of learning, creativity, communication skills, aesthetics, work motivation, work ethic of collaborative functioning and entrepreneurship-cum-social accountability. This will provide a firm foundation for building up a programme of 'Vocationalised Education' (to be distinguished from 'Vocational Education') at the secondary/ senior secondary stages.

- Vocational Education and Training (VET) may be conceived as a major national programme in the mission mode and be structurally and administratively placed outside the school system. VET in this new perspective will be built upon the bedrock of 10-12 years of work-centred education in the school system, unlike the prevailing notion of vocational education 'hanging' in vacuum. VET will include

  a) flexible and modular certificate/ diploma courses of varying durations;

  b) multiple entry and exit points with in-built credit accumulation facility;

  c) vertical and horizontal linkages with the academic, vocational and technical programmes;

d) accessibility all the way from the level of village clusters to the Block and District levels, and also in urban areas;

e) provision for carving out 'work benches' in the neighbourhood out of the existing economic activities, production and technical centres;

f) scope for engaging local farmers, artisans, mechanics, technicians, musicians, artists and other service providers as Resource Persons or invited faculty; and

g) a decentralised accreditation and equivalence programme which will also recognise 'work benches' for the purpose of evaluating and certifying students.

The Committee wishes to emphasise that the above proposal to institutionalise work-centred pedagogy in the school curriculum and building Vocational Education and Training as a programme of national significance for the adolescents and youth can be translated on the ground only if the necessary systemic changes are made. Let us not hesitate in fulfilling this historical expectation.

### *Common School System*

The Education Commission (1964-66) had recommended a Common School System of Public Education (CSS) as the basis of building up the National System of Education with a view to "bring the different social classes and groups together and thus promote the emergence of an egalitarian and integrated society." The Commission warned that "instead of doing so, education itself is tending to increase social segregation and to perpetuate and widen class distinctions." It further noted that "this is bad not only for the children of the poor but also for the children of the rich and the privileged groups" since "by segregating their children, such privileged parents prevent them from sharing the life and experiences of the children of the poor and coming into contact with the realities of life...... also render the education of their own children anaemic and incomplete."

The Commission contended that "if these evils are to be eliminated and the education system is to become a powerful instrument of national development in general, and social and national integration in particular, we must move towards the goal of a common school system of public education." The Commission also pointed out that such a system exists "in different forms and to varying degrees" in other nations like the USA, France and the Scandinavian countries. The British system, however, was based upon privileges and discrimination but, in recent decades, under democratic pressure, it has moved towards a comprehensive school system which is akin to the Common School System recommended by the Commission.

The 1986 policy, while advocating a National System of Education, resolved that "effective measures will be taken in the direction of the Common School System recommended in the 1968 policy." Taking into consideration these policy imperatives and the contemporary emphasis on decetralisation along with the necessary flexibility in the school system to be able to respond to the contextual curricular demands, the concept of the Common School System (CSS) has itself been evolving. There are two widespread misconceptions about CSS, often promoted by its detractors.

First, CSS is misperceived as a uniform school system. On the contrary, the Education Commission itself advocated that each institution should be "intimately involved with the local community...... be regarded as an individuality and given academic freedom." This guiding principle has assumed even greater significance in recent times in view of the expectation from each school or a cluster of schools to be able to respond to the local contexts and reflect the rich diversity across the country. Second, it is wrongly claimed that CSS will not permit a privately managed school to retain its non-government and unaided (or aided) character.

Again, on the contrary, CSS implies that all schools - irrespective of the type of their management, sources of income or affiliating Boards of examinations - will participate and fulfill their responsibility as part of the National System of Education. Based upon the evolving public discourse on CSS, the following definition of CSS can be constructed: Common school system essentially means a national system of education which is based on the values and principles of the Constitution of India and which provides education as a comparable quality to all children irrespective of their caste, creed, language, economic or cultural background, geographic location or gender. This is the perspective articulated by the National Policy on Education- 1986 and further elaborated by the National Curriculum Framework-2005.

Such a national system of education will be governed by certain minimum infrastructural, financial and curricular norms. For instance, in the context of the recruitment and working conditions of teachers, provision for basic resources, and structural flexibility and academic autonomy necessary for innovation are concerned with the spirit of National Policy on Education and the National Curriculum Framework 2005.

### *Three-Language Formula*

The three-language formula evolved out of a major political exercise and negotiations in the critical decade of 1950s and the early years of 1960s in response to the rising tensions with respect to different language regions of the country and the question of related cultural identities. In essence, this outcome reflected the federal spirit of our Constitution and the commitment to sustain and promote India's plural character. It is in this background that the 1986 policy made a commitment to implement the three-language formula "more energetically and purposefully." NCFSE-2005 also reiterates this position and proposes to make a renewed bid to fulfill the commitment.

While, as part of this formula, a crucial responsibility befalls upon the elementary stage of education to promote the mother tongue as a medium of education, it is the secondary/ senior secondary stage of education that becomes the real testing ground of the more challenging aspects of the formula. The 1986 policy also acknowledged the "uneven" implementation of the formula. The Hindi-speaking states, with their substantial demographic spread, have a special responsibility in responding to this challenge, especially with respect to the concept of the third language as a modern Indian language from a non-Hindi speaking region.

Concrete steps in this direction will provide a new thrust for the non-Hindi speaking states to make a fresh commitment to implement the language policy in letter and spirit. It is here that the political commitment made by the nation's leadership soon after independence to strengthen India's unity and integrity, promote inter-cultural dialogue and build an enlightened and articulate citizenship, will be redeemed.

### *Instructional Processes*

Curricular structure and course offerings are the necessary condition for quality secondary education. Instructional processes provide the sufficient condition for quality secondary education. Contemporary instructional processes and practices are characterised largely by lectures where students are passive listeners. Such instructional processes contribute at best to lower order cognition, memorisation and fragile learning; together, they make a grand nexus for large-scale failing in examination. Students lack problem-solving ability, higher order thinking and cognition, and creativity.

Most importantly, they miss out on 'learning to know' or learning to learn. If the new generation secondary education sets its targets for students to be able to think critically, solve problems individually and collectively, be creative, instructional processes must undergo a paradigm shift. Instructional processes must bring students at the centre of stage where they primarily learn to learn through peer interaction, problem-solving, experiential learning, etc. In this new instructional scenario, teachers will be facilitators of learning. Research as a tool for learning is quite common all over the world; introduced even at the pre-primary stage.

Indeed, by the time students are in the 9th and 10th standards they should become researchers to be able to crack problems, contemplate solutions, explore and experiments alternative and creative ways of problem-solving. In other words, instructional processes must be constructivist in its approach. Through constructivism, students will learn to construct their learning according to their own worldview that unfolds over the years of schooling. It is this learning to construct learning that will hold them in stead into the adult life at work and later.

Secondary education is the turning point for a large majority of students. Not only the certificate one earns after schooling but also the actual learning during schooling is the lifelong resource. Along with building dynamism in curricular framework as well as instructional processes, evaluation must undergo major changes. Conventionally, education system, particularly school education is guided and controlled by concern for results in examination irrespective of the quality of learning-whether fragile or sustainable.

The competition, though artificial, for securing percentage of marks in the final examination creates unusual stress in the students leading often to mental break down and suicides. This must change. Change in the mechanics of examination will be too simplistic a solution, amounting to treating the symptoms, not the disease itself. Examination-stress is directly related to facing the challenge of examination with 'fragile' learning due to memorising huge stock of information. In order to manage the stress factor in examination it will be necessary to ensure sustainable learning which the function of instructional processes is.

Yet, it will be necessary to reconstruct and redesign examination system with attributes like flexibility where a student can achieve mastery learning in a flexible time frame and accumulate credits; eliminating power tests (fixed duration), adopt continuous and comprehensive evaluation. The practice of mark sheets indicating marks in certain subjects must be replaced by a portfolio that would accommodate a student's performance in a variety of domains like life skills, academic/nonacademic and vocational subjects, personal qualities, etc. The portfolio should be comprehensive, revealing of the total being of the student.

Guidance and counselling play for meeting the needs of adolescent students going through the secondary and higher secondary stages of education. Provision for guidance and counseling is necessary in view of the fact that adolescent boys and girls are facing a fast process of socio-economic and cultural change, and quite often the traditional institutional frameworks provided by the family and community are not adequate for helping the adolescent to cope with the demands made upon him/her. In a society going through a rapid process of institutional change and modernisation, facilities for guidance and counseling in every secondary school are necessary.

Even as the secondary education system expands towards universalisation, staff for guidance and counseling will be required to ensure that first generation school goers receive adequate coverage in terms of their psychological and personality related needs. Financial allocation necessary for making guidance and counseling a common reality of every secondary school will need to be worked out, and institutional infrastructure necessary for making professional input for such a facility will have to be put in place.

### *Disparities in Schooling Facility*

There is a lot of disparity in schooling facilities in various regions of the country. There are disparities among the private schools, among private and government schools in the same state, between schools in central sector like KVS, NVS, Tibetan Schools, Sainik Schools, etc. Also, there are no specific norms for secondary schools. No wonder, India hosts secondary schools with magnificent building, library, laboratories, massive computer labs, cricket academy when majority of the secondary schools languish in dire poverty and deprivation. It must be appreciated that just the four-wall classrooms and teachers as per norms will not make a quality school.

For providing universal and free access to quality secondary education, it is imperative that specially designed norms are developed at the national level and then disaggregated for each State/UT keeping in mind the geographical, socio-cultural, linguistic and demographic conditions of not just the State/UT but also, wherever necessary, of the Blocks. Also, the disparities among various categories of schools must be reduced. This will require planning of educational facilities, and management of educational services to be streamlined.

*Norms for secondary schools*

| | |
|---|---|
| Land | 2 to 4 acres |
| Constructed area | not more than 50% of the land area |
| Teachers | One for every 30 students to be steadily moved to 1:20; at least one for every |

| | |
|---|---|
| | subject area; qualified teachers for sports, games and physical education, music and art, |
| Facilities | One classroom for every 30 students |
| | One integrated junior science lab. (for Classes 6th to 8th) |
| | One Science lab each for physics, chemistry, biology, English Language, Geography, |
| | Mathematics for 9th to 12th grades |
| | Disabled friendly facilities like ramp, special toilets, classroom furniture, etc. |
| | Braille and sign language-related equipment/computer software |
| | SIT to receive EDUSAT programmes |
| | OHPs, LCD projector |
| | Musical instruments, Gym equipment, sports and games material |
| | Junior computer lab with 30 computers for 6th to 8th graders with internet connectivity |
| | Senior Computer lab. with 30 computers for 9th to 12th graders with internet connectivity |
| | Separate health/restrooms for boys and girls |
| | Separate cubicles for teachers with computing facilities - one computer for every 4 teachers with internet connectivity |
| | Safe drinking water facilities |
| | School canteen and stores |
| | Separate toilets for girls and boys, and staff |
| | Library with computer facilities and professionally qualified staff |
| | Separate offices of Principal and vice-principal |

with computer facilities

In Chinese schools, the computer centers are usually huge with 150 to 200 computers, VDUs nearly sunk into the desks; all with high band internet connectivity, probably served through a high power server.

Electricity

Telephone

School office for non-teaching staff with computer facilities

Hobby room (s) for developing creativity and life skills including music, art and paintings

Playgrounds - soccer, hockey, volleyball, basketball, badminton, tennis, preferably separate for girls

Indoor games facilities separately for girls and boys

Gymnasium separately for girls and boys

Gardens and Social Forestry

The norms may appear immediately to be utopian. But Committee considers it to be the necessary utopia. The norms listed above already exist in large number of Kendriya Vidyalayas. Many of the reputed private schools have facilities much more than what is laid out in the norm. For large majority of the secondary schools, particularly the government aided institutions in various states, however, the norms would appear to be an Utopia. This mirage of an 'utopia' is probably because large number of schools do not have these facilities.

The State did not reprioritise the national economy to mobilise adequate resources for creating such facilities in the government, local body or aided schools inspite of the commitment made in the 1986 policy that the public outlay on education shall "uniformly exceed 6 per cent of the national income" and the directive under Article 41 of the

Constitution to "make effective provision for securing right to.... education" subject to "limits of economic capacity and development" of the State. Yet, it is necessary because without these facilities diversified quality schooling through constructivist paradigm is impossible.

The Committee does not maintain that these facilities can be created here and now. These facilities can be developed over a period of time in a phased manner. It may begin with the minimum provision of additional classrooms and teachers, but must move on to laboratories, libraries, computer lab, sports and games facilities, art and culture facilities, etc. in phases. Yet, if funds are allocated at the expected level (6% of GDP and beyond), such facilities can be created in a shorter span of time. The capital investment in secondary education is massive, but entirely within the limits of economic capacity and development.

However, the school facilities are used for not more than four to five hours a day. Effort should be made to make better use of the schooling facility by running it in more than one shift wherever feasible. For example, it is quite common among the Delhi Government schools to use the same building for two shifts. The second important choice is to create large schools as proposed in PURA (providing urban facilities in rural areas) by the President of India wherever possible particularly in thickly populated rural and urban areas. The per student establishment cost of large schools are comparatively less than such costs for small schools.

## Future of Secondary Education

India is emerging as the fastest-growing economy in the world. Several international reviews predicted that 21st century belongs to India and China as much as 20th century belonged to the USA, and 19th century to Europe. Such international reviews also warn lot of pitfalls and landmines on the way. The success depends largely upon human resource development. Whereas, the Indian higher education provides leadership-manpower in various sectors of national life and economy, secondary education has emerged as the single largest provider of working people in all spheres of national productivity.

Secondary education is the minimum common denominator. At this critical juncture of Indian development, secondary education needs a fresh look and examination for several reasons.

a) To maintain and accelerate the pace of growth of Indian economy, it will be necessary to raise the minimum basic education for the population, preferably to 12 years of schooling as common in most of the Organisation for Economic Corporative and Development OECD and other developing countries.

b) In order to meet the challenge of globalisation, enrolment in higher education has to increase from the current about 6% to at least 20% of the concerned age group (compare this with 33 per cent in the OECD countries, 50% and universalisation of higher education in UK and USA respectively). According to estimates, the transition rate from higher secondary stage to the undergraduate programmes is almost 65 per cent; and that provides six per cent enrolment in higher education. Essentially, hence, higher education has to be supported by a larger constituency. Besides, quality of higher education is squarely dependent upon the quality of graduates from secondary education.

c) There is an increasing social demand for secondary education further accelerated by the massive emphasis on universal elementary education through SSA. Earliest by 2007 and more likely by 2010, the demand for secondary education will sky rocket in the country.

## Issues in Secondary Education

Universalisation of Secondary Education will need to fulfill three major criteria, namely, universal enrolment in the 9th and 10th grades, universal retention achieving zero dropout rate, and universal performance at a predetermined level, at least 60 per cent of the students of the 10th grade will achieve 60 per cent mastery over subjects and other learning tasks. Initial questions that need to be resolved are: achieving universal access, equity and social justice. Whereas universal access may be possible to achieve through expansion of schooling facilities in the formal and unconventional modes, special efforts will be required for achieving equity, social justice and performance of all the diverse groups of learners.

Universalisation of secondary education is a long journey. It cannot be achieved overnight, though success in SSA will substantially facilitate the process. It will take at least 15 years of committed effort in a mission mode approach; universal secondary education should be targeted to be achieved by 2020. Success in accomplishment of this goal will be determined by the quality of planning and execution backed by political will and support.

### *Secondary Education Management Information System (SEMIS)*

Planning of educational system must be based on reliable data and information. Unlike elementary education where comprehensive and reliable database has been developed, secondary education does not have such authentic data with annual updates. With years of work, NIEPA has been able to develop a mechanism to update data on a wide range of the variables in elementary education every year; it publishes District Report Cards indicating the state of elementary education in each of the 539 districts (2004) to be increased to about 575 districts by 2005; and the State Report Cards indicating the state of elementary education in different states. It has covered 25 major states; the effort is on to cover the remaining 10 smaller states and union territories.

The SEMIS right from the beginning must include data on out of school adolescence and early youth, particularly those who cannot participate in the formal conventional schools in stipulated hours in the day. A large number of them are engaged in productive labour in both rural and urban areas as can be seen from the wide gap between the number of adolescents in the relevant age cohort and number of enrolled students in secondary education. This is important since the universalisation of secondary education has been defined to ensure participation of all adolescence and youth in the age group 15 to 18, beginning with adolescents in the age group 15 and 16.

Another important consideration is the education of the 'Focus Groups' - girls, students from SC, ST and OBC Communities, and the (physically and mentally) challenged adolescents. As all these groups need special assistance and support, the SEMIS should specially provide for data capturing on these groups and also define mechanisms to monitor education of the focus groups. Also, this will facilitate building access, equality, relevance and structural parameters of secondary education to ensure universal secondary education among the focus groups.

Decentralised planning and management of elementary education under DPEP and SSA has made significant impact on moving towards the targets of UEE. There are lessons to learn. Planning for universal secondary education should, right from the beginning, be founded on decentralised planning. The first and foremost requirement for decentralised planning, besides the data and information on the ground realities would be projection of demand for secondary education.

Given the wide regional disparities in educational development, such national macro level projections would be of limited value, a positive tool for policy making. For meaningful planning of secondary education, projections must be done for each state with desegregation into districts and blocks, gender, caste, religious and linguistic background. For decentralised planning, such projections have to be made at meso and micro level namely, for each block and district. While generating decentralised projection of demand for secondary education at block, district and state levels, it is important to take into cognisance the educational needs of different linguistic groups residing in the state.

In certain districts, there is concentration of students from linguistic group other than the natural language of the state, e.g. large Hindi speaking population in Howrah town in West Bengal. The Census 2001 provides a detailed account of linguistic minorities in different Indian provinces as brought out by the Commission for Linguistic Minorities. The projection of demands for secondary education should also take into consideration special educational needs of different linguistic and cultural groups. Almost every board of secondary education conducts examination in several languages.

In order to achieve universal access, the secondary education facilities have to be expanded. The expansion has to be accomplished through three different strategies depending upon the situational requirement. These are:

a) setting up new schools where no secondary school exists in the defined habitation,

b) upgrading elementary schools into high schools by adding extra classrooms and other facilities, and

c) providing additional classrooms and other related facilities in the existing secondary schools to accommodate more students.

The financial implications for the three strategies are significantly different- most expensive is setting up new school and least is providing marginal support to the existing secondary schools for enhancing intake capacities. A few states have taken a policy decision to upgrade all elementary schools to high schools in phased manner. The policy expanded to the national level, an additional about 2.50 lakh high schools can be added to the existing number of secondary schools by upgrading the elementary schools. The choice among the three alternatives given above has to be situational and based on school mapping in each block.

There have been some important efforts in school mapping at elementary education at NIEPA. The expertise can be extended to secondary education. What is really necessary is to plot at the district and block levels the existing secondary and senior secondary schools. This should provide a sound basis for decisions about establishing new schools, upgradation of elementary schools, and lateral expansion of classrooms and facilities in the existing secondary schools. In the process, it will be necessary to revise the norms for establishing secondary schools. For example, existing norms are to provide a primary school within one kilometer distance, an elementary school within three kilometers and a secondary school within five kilometers.

These norms were developed keeping in mind the time and labour to walk to the school at a time when the roads and transport network was grossly underdeveloped. With considerable developments in the rural roads and transportation, the time and energy to travel has reduced substantially. For example, in the mid 1950s and 1960s, students took 75 to 90 minutes to cover five kilometers to school on foot through rugged village pathways sometimes through the fields and water logged patches. Same distance is covered now in bicycle through partly brick-laid, partly kuccha road in less than 30 minutes. This scenario is fairly common in very large part of the country.

Exceptions, however, will be necessary in difficult terrains and hilly tracts. In the urban areas, students travel 20 to 30 kilometers for quality schooling. PURA, a project to which a detailed reference has been made in the budget speech by the Finance Minister proposes large high quality schools with transport facilities in a cluster of villages rather than poor quality school within the vicinity. This needs serious consideration. However, importance of school mapping is in generating a responsiveness to differential needs of secondary education in different localities.

In urban and semi urban areas and in rural areas with reasonably well developed road connectivity and transportation, norms of distance should be relaxed to create viable large high quality schools. In the relatively remote, difficult hills and terrains, and underdeveloped areas, the norms of distance have to be reduced. Equally important is the concern for the education of girls, keeping in view the superstitions, social taboos, etc, that forbids girls to travel long distances and/or study in co-educational schools. The school mapping should also facilitate identifying needs for setting up residential schools in such areas. The main contention is that school mapping should not be done mechanically with distance as the sole criteria.

Every district must set up a set of criteria for school mapping that will facilitate universal access to secondary education. Another important mapping exercise has to be done is with respect to courses at the senior secondary level. The distribution of science stream as well as vocational courses is not as wide as courses in commerce and humanities streams. In order that the facilities for science and vocational education are equitably distributed it will be necessary to carry out course mapping in every district and block. The same norms for school mapping cannot be valid through out the country. Keeping the goal of universal secondary education, state and locale specific norms should be developed in consultation with the states. The mapping facility, now thrown open by the satellite launched by ISRO should be fully exploited.

As a follow-up to the mapping of schools and courses, and the projection of demands, the next stage of planning is assessment of physical infrastructure and educational facilities, namely the additional classrooms and new schools in such habitations where secondary schools are not available at a reasonable distance. Further, physical infrastructure cannot be restricted to additional classrooms; it must include associated infrastructure for all round development of the students like play grounds, gyms, etc. Such exercises have to be done necessarily at block level or even at the sub-block level. This should provide the actual requirement of required infrastructure in each district and the state for further planning of financial requirement, teacher requirement, etc.

The assessment of physical infrastructure can be greatly facilitated by SEMIS as experienced in DISE for elementary schools. Mere lateral expansion of secondary schooling facilities can serve the purpose of only universal (physical) access. The provision of extra classrooms and teachers will not ensure quality, nor would it contribute to the concept of schooling described earlier. In order to provide quality education and life skills to the students, all schools have to be upgraded qualitatively. This is true for the existing secondary and senior secondary schools as well as the new ones to be established.

Such facilities at the minimum will include provision for laboratories, library and learning resources, information technology resources, audiovisual facilities including SITs support educational delivery through EDUSAT, facilities for sports and games, and cultural activities. For providing quality secondary education, it will be necessary to develop norms for schools. While there should be a core set of national norms, these norms have to be further elaborated and developed with locale specificity in each state, district and blocks in consultation with the states.

### *Open Learning System*

Irrespective of expansion of educational facilities in

secondary schooling, all the adolescence and youth in the concerned age group will not be able to take advantage of formal schooling in stipulated hours of the day that often coincide with the productive labour required in the rural areas for agriculture and in urban areas for a variety of income generating activities particular for the lower middle-class and poor families. It will be necessary to design, create and establish alternative educational provisions for such prospective learners. Besides the National Institute of Open Schooling, several states have established open schools providing comparable quality of education with that in the formal schools.

The open school network has to be expanded to ensure that every State provides open schooling facility through regional languages. The existing open schools depend largely upon the print material and personal contact programmes through the formal schools. A large majority of the open school students are unable to take advantage of personal contact programmes and counseling services; they primarily depend upon the print material which often varies in quality. It will be necessary to enhance quality of open schooling through a variety of measures, particularly the counseling and tutorial services. A great opportunity has been opened by the launching of the educational satellite in September 2004.

The video-conferencing facility can provide virtual classroom facility for school education through regional languages through state channels. In order to ensure that open schooling derives full advantage of the videoconferencing facilities as a compliment to counseling and tutorial services through EDUSAT, all the secondary and senior secondary schools that serve as study centre must be equipped with satellite interactive technology (SIT) facilities. Also, DTH delivery of education through cable network should be explored. This opens a new area of planning along with decentralised planning for formal secondary schools. It will be necessary to plan for open schooling provision in every state.

The open learning system at higher education comprising open universities and distance education departments in the dual mode universities cater to the educational needs of more than 20% students in higher education. The open school network when fully developed should be able to cater to at least 15% students in secondary education. Second shift (evening shift) school for working youth should also be considered wherever feasible.

### *Teacher Requirement*

Teachers are the most significant element in secondary education. Based on the projection of demand for secondary education, an important and necessary exercise will be the projection of requirement of additional teachers for universal secondary education. With the upgradation of courses and contents, secondary education particularly in science, mathematics and certain departments of social sciences, require specialist teaching faculty. As a result, the teacher-student ratio may not be the right criteria for assessing teacher requirement. Equally true is the non-applicability of classroom-teacher ratio in secondary education.

The teacher requirement is to be based on requirement of subject specialists in different schools; the teacher-student ratio and teacherclassroom ratio can form the complementary criteria for determining the requirement of teachers. For decentralised planning at the district and block levels, the teacher requirement should be assessed at the block level accumulated at the district level. This will facilitate developing teachers as a district level cadre.

### *Block and District Plan*

The actions mentioned above should provide adequate

inputs to develop district and block level plan of expansion of secondary education with relevant facilities for upgradation of quality of secondary education. The first and foremost requirement is to develop district and block specific plan of development of secondary education spread over the next 15 years — 2005 to 2020. Such decentralised plan at the district and block levels should indicate development in different phases e.g. development plans for the remaining years of the 10th Five-year plan, and then projected further into relevant 11th through 13th Five year plans.

However, such plans need to be reviewed from time to time in the midterm evaluation format as practised now. It will be necessary to carry out annual review as the expansion of secondary education facilities for universal access enters the last phase nearing 2020. For, Universalisation of Secondary Education will be increasingly difficult as one move from the first to the last mile situations.

Universal secondary education can be achieved only with universal retention and quality. The transition rates from 8th to 9th and 9th to 10th grades are more than 90 per cent. The estimated dropout rate between 9th and 10th is less than 10%. However, there is a massive failure at the board examination, often more than 50 per cent, that too after stringent scrutiny at the pre-board examination. As a result, the accumulated success rate is less than 40 per cent of those who enter the 9th standard. For universalisation of secondary education this must change.

The key to change is locked in the quality of schooling. Since teachers are the most important component of quality schooling, it will be necessary to continuously upgrade the quality of teachers through on-the-job training, inservice education programmes and a variety of other mechanisms, besides preservice qualifying programme of teacher training (B.Ed.). There is great regional disparity in the provision for secondary teacher training institutions in the country. There are regions, north-eastern region for example, do not have enough teacher training facilities compared to say Maharashtra, Karnataka and other such states where there are large number of private teacher training institutions.

Careful state level planning will be necessary for ensuring steady supply of trained teachers and their continuous upgradation. Such state specific planning must also be supported with dependable projections of teacher requirements with various subject specialisations. The International Commission on Education for 21st Century (UNESCO) indicated that work-training-work-training cycle is more effective than long preservice education of teachers. While the emphasis is on inservice education of the teachers for quality improvement, it is important to recognise that the conventional in-service education provided by the teacher education institutions do not actually contribute to the development of relevant skills and attitudes for quality improvement in instruction and student learning.

Besides the conventional in-service education programmes, it will be necessary to develop a mechanism whereby secondary school teachers will able to share their experiences and learn from each other, indeed develop a learning community and culture. There are lots to learn from the experiences in BRC and CRCs in SSA in this regard. The shift in the process and strategy of teacher upgradation has to be professionalised by developing a blueprint for development of each teacher in each school collated at the block level so that teachers of similar development needs may be provided with specific focused training and development inputs.

Many of the State governments have adopted the policy of recruiting para teachers as a cost saving alternative to regular professionally qualified fully paid teachers. In some of the states, teaching has been declared as a dying cadre. This is a dangerous trend with short-term relief at the cost of long-term debilitating effect on the education system. No society can simultaneously deprofessionalise teachers yet educate its children and ensure the future. The considered opinion of the committee is to appoint professionally qualified teachers with full salary and benefits.

Accordingly, the cost projections on teachers have been calculated; the norm practised in the Kendriya Vidyalay Sangathan has been the basis. Even at the risk of repetition, the committee refers to flag that is with the allocation of 6% GDP to the education sector, it would be possible to recruit fully qualified teachers with full salary and benefits. Any compromise on this issue will be at the risk of the future of the nation. Heads of schools hold the key to quality management and self-renewal of schools. This is borne out by empirical research all over the world during the last five decades. It is important to recognise that managing and leading schools is a specialist job.

It is not an automatic extension of activities of a teacher, although teaching skills and experience helps. Heads of schools must be provided professional training in management of schools of six months duration, preferably with three months of practice/practical training in the pattern of diploma in educational planning and management offered by NIEPA. However, like teachers, diploma education in school management of the headmasters with short term training every three to five years. Over the years, inspection and supervision has been dysfunctional. With the expansion of educational facilities - schools and teachers - there was no corresponding increase in the supervising personnel.

A few inspectorate staff is involved in a large variety of administrative work. Academic supervision has become a thing of the past. This must change. Quality universal secondary education warrants a well developed system of inspection and supervision. The inspectorate staff must be increased. Importantly, the supervisory personnel must be provided with professional training in scientific practices in inspection and supervision.

## Financial Projections

A few statements outlining the financial policy and management are important.

1. The requirement for universal elementary education is estimated at about 3.0% of GDP. Together, 5.13% of GDP per year would be adequate for universal elementary and secondary education. The review of the performance of UPA government has flagged its dissatisfaction over nonallocation of promised 6% of GDP to education. This raises the hope that allocation of 6% GDP may not be very far away.

2. The financial allocation should be phased out. To begin with, the State will ensure availability of classrooms on teachers in every school. This should be followed by library, laboratory, sports and games facility, et cetera. Target should be to move towards the norm of secondary schooling over the next 10 years.

3. About 25% secondary schools are private non-aided that do not receive any government grant. However, these private non-aided schools provide educational coverage to only 8.72% children (according to VIth All India survey data; VII the survey data are awaited). Compared to that percentage of students in private aided schools are above 46%. These privately run schools comprise nonprofit society/trust managed institutions, schools established by entrepreneurial motivations, and large chain of schools being set up by international initiatives. The right to establish schools is guaranteed by the Indian Constitution. However, as can be seen, government provides for secondary education of more than 90% students.

Less than 10% students in private schools are from the creamy layer of the society. Although the number of privately run schools and percentage of students being covered by such schools are increasing, they would not be able to cater to the educational needs of today's out-of-school children who have to be schooled back for universalisation of secondary education. And, government must provide for their education. Although the 'creamy layer' can be asked to bear their educational costs reducing the financial burden on the government allowing it to divert the educational resources for those who cannot afford, the current pattern of growth of private participation does not indicate any significant relief to needed financial commitment of the government. The three cardinal principles for universal secondary education are:

a) the government must ensure that no child is deprived of educational facility because of financial incapability,

b) no student is financially exploited; and

c) schooling is not used for commercial purposes as pronounced by the Supreme Court judgment.

4. Open schooling has traditionally been a cheaper alternative of education. More importantly, open scooters, despite their comparatively poor economic background, pay full cost of their education. Both are unacceptable; they do not stand the test of equity and social justice. Open schooling should receive full state support to ensure high-quality education and non-exploitation of the students. However, because of large enrolment, open learning system achieves economy of scale. The financial policy for opens schooling should be full financial support for quality education allowing and encouraging benefits of economy of scale.

5. Education is in the concurrent list and secondary education has largely been in the domain of the state governments. However, leaving universalisation of secondary education in the states will not make much headway. State governments already spend on an average about 22 per cent of the annual budget on education alone. Further, estimated 92 per cent of the total state expenditure on secondary education is the salary cost. Given the financial situation in the states, they will not have adequate fund for supporting expansion of secondary education and quality upgradation. Financing of universal secondary education must be a collective responsibility of the centre, state and the community (social financing).

6. With a centrally sponsored scheme, central government should fund the capital expenditure for building and quality upgradation facilities; additional teacher cost at least for the remaining period of 10th plan and the 11th plan, capacity building of teachers and headmasters, as well as research and development associated with universalisation of secondary education. State component should share the burden of recurring expenditure.

7. The centre-state sharing of financial burden should be in the pattern of SSA - 85:15 till end of 10th plan, and 75: 25 till the end of 11th plan. However, for the special category of states covered under Schedule 6 of the Constitution, central aid should be 100% till end of the 11th plan; 90:10 there after till the end of 12th plan. The cost of universalisation of secondary education in the backward regions defined under schedule 5 of the Constitution in states other than those covered under schedule 6 should also be provided fully by the central government till end of 11th plan and 90:10 till end of the 12th plan.

8. Because of large-scale mobilisation of elementary education due to success in SSA the pressure on

secondary education is already being perceived. the pressure would be significantly high by 2007. The funding support for secondary education must begin with the financial year 2006-2007, preferably at the RE stage of 2005-2006.

# 4

# Mobility and Motivation

A comparison of salaries of staff and management in relation to corresponding certified courses in technical areas and management areas indicates that employers are not looking for certification or relevant technical writing educational qualifications while hiring or while designing the compensation package. Project management certification appears to hold some value, as salaries for those with training in this area are higher than for managers without training.

Based on the fact that, out of the largest respondent base, 0% have a technical communication-related education, the market could assume that formal education in the field is not of paramount importance in the current scenario. The current scenario being, increased outsourcing to India generating quick jobs requires writers who can adapt to the technical communication profession's requirements. This means India would not be growing a profession where the majority of technical writers are trained professionals. The number of respondents who obtained on-the-job training indicates the same trend.

## Education and Compensation

If the team size and average salary for team members of a particular sized team speak at all, it appears that the average salary that an organisation with a larger technical communication team size is somewhat higher. For a team size of 50-100, for example, the average salary is Rs. 505,467 per annum, while for a team size of 2-5, the average salary is Rs. 442,357, per annum. Looking at the statistics, we can infer that the larger the team of technical communicators, the better the compensation and benefits package.

Increasing requirements for technical communicators in India have obviously seen the growth of technical communication service providing companies. It would be interesting to find out if their clients are mainly IT companies from outside or within India. While the IT services and IT product companies average the highest salary per year, it is startling to note that technical communication service providing companies fall lower in the pay scale, with an average of Rs. 202,908 per annum.

A crucial aspect about the growth of technical writing as a high-end, respected, sought-after profession in India is the work opportunities that this profession offers to people in the field. If the profession continues to offer tasks like managing and updating existing documents, or creating new documents, as the main activity, professional growth may stagnate. 77.7% and 82.6% of respondents, correspondingly, perform these activities. It appears that information design, information architecture, documentation strategy, consulting, developing documentation solutions, and similar activities are still not under the purview of outsourced technical documentation activities to a country like India.

If senior technical communicators have to grow, the latter responsibilities are what they would be looking to take up. This would be an interesting question to ask those who have ambitions in this direction. Finding talent in India can be incredibly difficult. While there are a number of under- and un- employed high school and college graduates in India, generally these individuals are not trained with the skills needed by multinational employers. Indians with strong skills may not fit the needs of multinational employers because of the historical variations in work practices from those found in the West.

In other words, while at some levels and in some industries there are many candidates with the technical skills to fill a position, they may not have the cultural skills to "fit in" with an organisation. Finally, there is a shortage of talent at the upper end of the employment scale, particularly in IT. Turnover levels have gone up in many industries, including IT and IT enabled sectors and to a lesser extent in advertising, marketing, and retailing. Though still below the rate of comparable industry segments in the West, turnover can be a problem, as economic growth, increased salaries, and a shortage of skilled employees at the top of the scale can tempt the best and the brightest to change jobs often.

As a result of this shortage, and to combat turnover rates, salaries have risen dramatically in high demand sectors, especially at the upper ends of the scale. In addition, salaries in India account for less than half the value of a typical compensation package. Benefits like rent-free or concessional housing, free use of motor vehicles and/or drivers, interest subsidies on loans, and the like may all be part of a total compensation package.

## Compensation

Although pay in India is considerably lower than in Western countries (and even some developing nations), shortages of skilled workers (especially in IT) have led to dramatic pay inflation. Salaries in some sectors of the economy climbed at a staggering 40 percent annually during the mid-1990s. Since then, the Asian financial crisis and the IT slowdown have caused the economy to cool off, with the job market following suit. Consequently, pay increases have slowed markedly over the past few years, although average salary increases continue to significantly outpace the inflation rate of 6-7%.

The best entry-level employees with a high-tech degree from one of India's well-renowned Indian Institute of Technology campuses can expect an annual salary of around US$14-16,000. While this sum is substantially more than it was five years ago, it seems startlingly inexpensive when compared to the offers that some of these same graduates receive from companies overseas. Entry-level employees from second-tier schools receive lower levels of compensation.

Less skilled employees and those in other industries, such as the medical transcriptionists employed by multinationals who have discovered the cost-advantages of remote processing in the sub-continent, receive about $1,200 per year (this level is fast increasing), while the same job in the US would command more than twenty times as much pay (about $25,000). Depending on the industry and job function, employees higher up the corporate ladder in middle management can expect to receive an annual salary range up to about $US30,000. Senior level employees can expect base salaries ranging from about $35,000 to $85,000 depending on the function and the industry of the employee.

The basic salary of an employee in India usually accounts for between 40 and 50 percent of the total package, meaning benefits or "allowances" are an important part of compensation in India. This is partly because there have traditionally been tax advantages to receiving payment in kind. Proposed changes in India's tax rules will eliminate many of these tax advantages, which will present a significant compensation challenge for HR professionals in India. However, at this time, benefits still account for a significant part of any employment package, and thus continue to play vital role in luring and retaining key employees.

In addition, certain perquisites like housing, cars, and loans (companies often offer their employees very low interest short and long term loans) will continue to be taxed at concessional rates, even after the new tax rules are enacted, and thus will remain in demand by employees. Among the most significant benefits is housing. Employers often reimburse a portion of the rental costs of the employee in the form of house rent allowance (HRA), a portion of which is not subject to income tax.

Another important benefit is the medical allowance. Medical allowances may come in a variety of forms. Companies may reimburse expenditures incurred by the employee for his own or his family's medical treatment, pay a fixed allowance for routine check-ups, or undertake a group medical insurance policy. Pay packets may also include a "dearness" allowance, or as it is known in the US, a cost of living adjustment. Other examples of allowances include work clothing allowances, professional education allowances, commuting allowances, holiday allowances, and the like.

For expatriates, allowances may include the entire family's airfare on home leave, and the fares of children studying abroad and visiting their parents in India. Because of poor road conditions and slow traffic, a car with a driver is generally necessary for expatriates who are unaccustomed to such driving conditions. Drivers and cars are necessary for senior level Indian managers as well. Other benefits that might help to attract or retain professionals include gymnasium facilities, child-care facilities, periodical subscriptions, club memberships, insurance and loan facilities.

Once a firm manages to find and hire a top employee, retention becomes the key issue. This is most important in the IT industry, where the majority of India's job hoppers are employed. The famed International Technology Park in Bangalore, which boasts self-contained power facilities, modern gymnasiums, food courts and other amenities, is indicative of what it takes to retain IT professionals. In a country where thousands of villages are without electricity or telephones, India's technology parks stand out as bastions of unexpected affluence.

The most favored employers will make a significant investment in training their employees. Although some might contend that training simply makes the employees more saleable, it is equally likely to breed employee loyalty. This is especially true in the IT sector, where skills quickly become dated and employees need constant retraining in order to remain current. Indeed, a Business Today / Hewitt Associates study rated Infosys, a company that puts all of its junior employees through a three-month training program, the most favored employer in India. All good companies provide other facets of employee development, including skills upgrade training and personal development programs on a regular, on-going basis.

In addition, maintaining job satisfaction through variation of duties is important to ensure that employees don't simply leave out of boredom. New Delhi-based Hughes software, for example, has initiated an internal placement program that helps employees to move between departments and projects within the company. Although this has caused some logistical problems, as some projects lose valued personnel, the cost to the company may well be lower than losing the employee to a competitor.

## Job Market

Stocks and shares is a method to raise funds from the public for use by the government or private companies. Until a couple of decades, Mumbai was India's first and only stock exchange and few industries were listed in the share market. Today, there is a stock exchange in every metropolitan city, where business worth crores takes place everyday. Capital market experts are qualified industry specialists who advise on buying and selling of stocks. The industry provides work to economists, accountants, financial analysts, industry specialists, capital market specialists, investment and financial planners, financial specialists and other such professionals. Firms in this business are generally organised into three departments. These include:

— sales and trading for the owners of securities;

— investment banking for the firms and governments that issue securities;

— capital markets, which fall in between the other two divisions.

Capital markets specialists are employed by mutual funds and financial investment companies to keep track of emerging trends in the markets and work on capital decisions in the light of these trends. Securities analysts are employed by investment advisers, brokerage firms, banks, insurance companies and other large financial institutions to give correct information on industries and markets. A Securities analyst is usually an economics/commerce graduate.

Investment management involves dealing with analysis of the growth of an industry, the economic policies related to industrial financing, monitoring and review for sound financial management of resources. Some firms appoint security representatives who have varied duties, like opening accounts for new customers, obtaining all the information required to permit the customer to buy and sell securities through the brokerage firm.

There are also jobs for marketing and sales representatives of security and investment firms specialising in specific areas such as handling institutional accounts or even in bond issues or mutual funds. To enter this field it is important to understand the working of the stock exchange and money markets thoroughly. Different exchanges in the country today have different norms. So, it is essential to be knowledgeable on how it functions. Most firms also prefer to take on MBA's with a specialisation in finance, or postgraduates with specialised training in capital markets, stocks and securities or other courses in financial management. With professional qualification, you can either join a stock broking firm or stock exchange, or even open your own financial agency.

This is inclusive of both, the membership fee and the security deposit. This fee varies from time to time, depending on the status of the market. It also varies from one city to the other at any given point of time. Besides this, two years' experience in the securities market is also required. The national stock exchange has introduced an online facility for testing and certification. It tests the practical knowledge and skills required to operate in the financial markets.

The entire process of testing, assessing and scoring is fully automated, and anyone who has completed plus two is eligible for the exam. A degree in commerce/economics is required to be eligible for the postgraduate courses in stocks and securities, capital markets, and other programmes in financial management. Postgraduate programmes in capital market studies, and in stocks and securities are available in select universities and institutes in the country. Moreover, postgraduate courses in economics and commerce are available in most universities in the country.

It is necessary to have a sound knowledge of finance, be informed on every industry and keep abreast with the ups and downs of the market. Equity Research is a very specialised finance field, requiring either an MBA in finance or a chartered accountancy qualification. And apart from all the academic and financial requirements, to be in the capital markets business, you must have a feel for the market; knowledge, interest, a knack for learning about stocks and shares; and an analytical, logical mind.

You must also have the powers of good judgment; tact in dealing with clients; and plenty of business acumen. The commodity being traded here is large volumes of money, not only in terms of the money involved, but the volatility of the shares being traded. Stocks and securities is therefore a profession with a higher risk profile than others, and your professional growth, to a large extent, depends on the share market, over which one has little control.

If you are good at your work, there are plenty of jobs waiting for you. You may choose to work in the Stock exchanges; or at the Securities and Exchange Board of India (SEBI); with financial institutions; with investment banks; or you can also open your own financial consulting agency. Twenty per cent of our traditional banks also now own full-service brokerage firms. Stock broking is truly a profession of the new millennium. With more and more money being traded by the second, there is now a great demand for trained professionals.

## Higher Education

The recent proposals to cut the fees charged by IITs and IIMs by as much as 80 percent are supposed to create equitable access to quality education for the poor. The goal is meritorious, the proposed instrument is wrong. Delivering quality education is expensive. Among other things, colleges need teachers who are as intelligent, knowledgeable, motivated, and inspired as their students. They must be able to attract the very best minds to the teaching profession to educate the next generation. Without powerful economic incentives, the talented will not pursue PhD degrees and teaching careers. There is no way around this large expense.

Until quite recently, most of the cost was borne by the taxpayer through government subsidy to colleges and universities. The subsidy enabled the poor have access to inexpensive higher education but the government budget could support only a limited number and size of such institutions. A country of a billion people needs hundreds, not a dozen, centers of excellence in higher education. The IITs admit a mere one or two percent from a highly talented pool of applicants. Behind this proud statistic lies a painful truth: our educational policy shuts the door of opportunity on some 98 percent who do not get in. Many of those who have the money pay some twenty to fifty lakh rupees go abroad to get a degree, and rarely come back.

The poor do not have the money to go abroad, and the government does not have the money to subsidise a hundred IITs. Higher fees mobilize private resources to build additional educational capacity. Lower fees for the poor and educational loan programs are the two widely used devices for addressing the problem of access to education. Lower fees for the poor place the administrative burden of determining the individual student's ability-to-pay on college officials, often inviting corruption.

Colleges can use some difficult-to-manipulate indicators to assess the financial means of students. For example, a student who paid fifty thousand rupees a year to attend an elite secondary school must make an exceptionally convincing case to qualify for lower college fees. Education loans offer a simpler, widely used, solution. Commercial banks give loans for education subject to admission and good academic standing at approved colleges. Students get to choose the institution they wish to attend and pay for, imposing certain discipline on college administration.

Given the level of compensation commanded by the graduates of IITs and IIMs, the obligation to pay the loan with interest does not cause their students to forego their educational opportunities. An efficiently run, and widely available system of education loans effectively addresses the problem of access for the poor. If the government must provide subsidies, it can do so by reducing the interest charged on such loans by one or two percentage points.

It is unwise to provide government guarantees for such loans because guarantees invite abuse by the unscrupulous individuals and institutions. Self-financing of higher education through higher fees and student loans allows the limited resources of government to be focused on subsidising newer educational institutions in areas and disciplines where market forces have not yet developed. Some half-a-century ago, visionary governments squeesed their tight budgets to create and subsidise a few institutions of higher education in technology and management-fields that were new at that time.

India's growing ability to compete in the world markets is the fruit of that foresight. Nations of the world compete by the quality and size of the educational systems. Many are watching with a touch of envy as India captures a chunk of the information and communications technology markets. If India stumbles by failing to use its limited educational budget productively-to create new "seed farms" for future talent-it will be left behind in the race.

Reducing fees for higher education is bad policy. Financing education by bank loans to fee-paying students lets the existing colleges increase their capacity for quality higher education for the rich as well as the poor. Such a policy will enable India to build its human capital to compete in the knowledge economy. Educational institutions that are able and willing to finance themselves should not be forced to beg for handouts from Delhi. The proposal to cut their fees appears to be an exercise in bureaucratic and political control masquerading as access for the poor.

Implementation of the proposal will starve these institutions of funds, tighten bureaucratic grip on their operations, drive away talent from the teaching profession, and slow down the expansion of higher education. History will not be kind to those who play games with the future of the nation.

## Compensation for Teacher Education

With one in four teachers absent at a typical government-run primary school, India has the second-highest average absence rate among the eight countries for Within India, the absence rate ranged from 15 percent in Maharashtra to 42 percent in Jharkand. Absence rates are generally higher in lowincome states: doubling per capita income is associated with a 4.7 percentage point lower predicted absence. The rates of teaching activity among the teachers who are present are lower in higher-absence states and schools. In some states, only 20 to 25 percent of teachers were engaged in teaching at the time of the visit.

Absence rates are considerably higher than could be accounted for by official non-teaching duties, such as staffing polling stations during elections or conducting immunisation campaigns, which are sometimes cited as important causes of absence. Based on the responses of each school's head teacher or primary respondent, official non-teaching duties account for only about 4 percent of total absences. In other words, on any given day, only about 1 percent of primary teachers are absent because they are carrying out official non-teaching-related duties.

Preliminary calculations by the authors suggest that 8-10 percentage points of absence could potentially be attributed to annual leave, medical leave and other officially sanctioned reasons. This implies that variation across states in "excess" absence may be considerably greater than variation in raw absence rates. Higher teacher salaries do not seem to be associated with lower teacher absence. Head teachers are 4-5 percentage points more likely to be absent than regular teachers. Since absence increases with all three of these variables, it is likely that betterpaid teachers are more absent.

Similarly, although regular teachers are typically paid much higher salaries than contract teachers, there is no significant difference in absence between the two groups. Finally, since nominal teacher salaries are very similar across states, relative teacher salaries are higher in poorer states and yet poorer states have higher absence rates. One reason why higher pay is not associated with lower absence may be that teachers feel little risk of being fired for absence. Only 1 head teacher in nearly 3000 public schools reported ever dismissing a teacher for repeated absence.

While few teachers are subject to much risk of being fired, the costs and benefits of attending school on a given day could vary among teachers depending on working conditions, as well as on their vulnerability to sanctions. The vulnerability of teachers to these sanctions presumably depends both on the monitoring regime and on the teacher's level of power. Power differentials may explain the higher absence rates of older, more educated, and more experienced teachers, as well as the finding that males are significantly more absent than females.

Non-pecuniary factors other than working conditions could also affect teachers' costs and benefits of attending school. Teacher absence is considerably lower in schools with better infrastructure, a potentially important element of working conditions. Under this specification, each point on the index is associated with a 1.0 to 1.5 percentage point reduction in the probability of absence-so that moving from 0 to 5 on the index reduces the predicted absence rate by 5.0 to 7.5 points.

Since one of the ways in which better teachers might be rewarded is through better postings (to schools with superior infrastructure), we also test this relationship using only the teachers who are on their first posting; we find that better infrastructure is still significantly associated with lower teacher absence. Other working conditions that might be expected to affect teacher motivation are the remoteness of the school and the teaching conditions. Anecdotal evidence shows that many teachers prefer less remote schools. In our data, teachers in schools that are far from a paved road are nearly 4 percentage points less likely to be in school than those closest to a road.

Although inspections in India are often considered toothless, teachers in schools that had been inspected in the 3 months prior to the visit were about 2 percentage points less likely to be absent. Because school inspections may not be allocated randomly , we also test an alternative measure of inspection intensity: the fraction of the schools in a district that have been inspected recently. Moving from a district with no inspections in the past 3 months to one where every school has been inspected in the past 3 months is associated with a seven percentage point lower level of teacher absence.

The addition of state fixed effects makes this result insignificant, however, raising the possibility that the average inspection variable may be picking up the general quality of educational administration in the state. Local communities could potentially provide an alternative source of monitoring. One way to interpret the lower absence rates in schools with more educated parents and high pupil-teacher ratios is that local monitoring is more effective when parents are more educated and more parents could potentially complain about absence.

Similarly schools with PTAs that have met in the past three months have lower absence. This could reflect either the importance of local community monitoring or a tendency for more conscientious teachers and headmasters to organise PTA meetings. While a priori reasoning suggests local monitoring could potentially affect teacher behavior, the regressions do not provide much guidance about how policies could reduce absence by strengthening ties between schools and local communities.

The duration of a teacher's posting at the school has no significant relationship with absence. Absence rates in non-formal schools, which are staffed by teachers from the community, are higher than in regular government schools. Schools with and without parent-teacher associations have similar absence rates.

It is worth considering the implications of alternative forms of contractual arrangement. Contract teachers in the public system have much lower wages, are presumably easier to dismiss, and have similar level of absence. Private schools similarly have much lower wages than public-school teachers, but also a greater chance of dismissal for absence. Private-school teachers are only a little less likely to be absent than publicschool teachers in general, but are 8 percentage points less likely to be absent than public-school teachers in the same village.

Mechanically, this is because private schools are disproportionately located in villages with particularly high absence rates in government schools. Advocates of private schools may interpret the correlation between the presence of private schools and weakness of public schools as suggesting that private schools spring up in areas where government schools are performing particularly badly, while opponents may argue that the entry of private schools leads to exit of politically influential families from the public school system, and further weakens pressure on public-school teachers to attend school.

A 10 percent increase in teacher absence is associated with 1.8 percent lower student attendance, as well as with a 0.02 standard deviation reduction in test scores on a simple 14-question test given to a sample of 4th-grade children. These coefficients are robust to controls but small in magnitude. They may underestimate the impact of teacher absence for two reasons, however.

First, measurement error in estimating absence rates for the relevant teachers will attenuate the coefficients downward. Second, if marginal students drop out of school in response to high teacher absence rates, those students who remain in school may have different background characteristics than students in schools with lower teacher absence.

# 5

# Life Style Related Issues and Work Environment

The new era of globalisation of the late 20th century and early 21st century has seen an increase in the international mobility of highly-skilled, talented individuals (i.e. human capital) as new job opportunities for high-skill individuals are opened by globalisation. The topic of human capital mobility and brain drain has remained somewhat dormant in the academic and policy literature in the last two to three decades after being actively debated in the 1960s.

The international movement of human capital (HC) can be identified, in practice, as the movement of scientists, engineers (e.g. in the information sector), executives, and other professionals across frontiers. These are people with special talents, high skills and specialised knowledge in the scientific, technological and cultural areas. Another dimension of the international mobility of talent is entrepreneurial migration, say people with talent for business creation and resource mobilisation rather than necessarily individuals with a high stock of formal education.

From the viewpoint of developing countries (and transition economies) the international mobility of HC has been seen with a mix of concern and possibility. The internationalists favored unrestricted international migration of highly skilled individuals as a vehicle to enhance "global efficiency," while the "nationalists" were concerned with the adverse impact on national development of human capital outflows to advanced economies. In the world of the early 21 century the debate is better framed in terms of the contribution of international mobility of human capital to global knowledge creation and dissemination, global inequality, national development and successful post-socialist transition.

On the one hand developing countries encourage national students to earn graduate degrees abroad in science, technology and other disciplines as a way to upgrade their knowledge and human resource base. On the other hand, when outstanding scientists and professionals stay abroad, the concern arises of a "brain drain" due to the flight of scarce human capital and talent whose contribution is needed for economic development at home.

## International Mobility of Human Capital

The demand for skilled individuals has been on the rise in the last decade or so. The main pole of attraction for foreign skilled people is the United States. Some 40 percent of its foreign -born population have tertiary education levels. Since the early 1990s some 900,000 skilled professionals mainly Informational Technology (IT) specialists have emigrated to the United States coming from India, China, Russia and some OECD countries. These immigrants often come under the H1-B visa program for highly skilled professionals.

The magnitude and impact on developing countries of the outflow of human capital varies from region to region. In Africa, the International Organisation for Migration (IOM), estimates that around 300,000 professionals live and work in Europe and North America. Casual evidence shows that as a consequence of the large scale emigration of medical doctors in Africa, the poor are forced to seek medical treatment from traditional healers while the rich elite fly to London for their routine medical checkups.

This emigration of professionals in Africa has several adverse effects such as reducing the stock of scarce human capital at home, the erosion of the domestic tax base, the failure to form a middle-class of educated people, a stabilising factor in most societies. In higher per capita income developing countries the consequences of the outflow of human capital could to be less dramatic.

In India, however, in the year 2000, it was estimated that some 1,500 highly qualified Indians returned from the United States, although more than 30 times that number depart each year. The outflow of human capital is not only led by better opportunities for study and work in the developed countries (pulling factors) but also by economic and political conditions at home (pushing factors).

### *Science and Technology Resources*

Range from the definition of science, which in the Anglo-Saxon world is meant to cover only natural sciences (physics, biology, etc.) to the non-reporting of research and development expenditure in poorer developing countries that makes more difficult international comparisons. Intertemporal and international comparisons of resources devoted to science and technology in former socialist countries and western economies is also difficult due to different definitions of S&T activities (and national output) used during the socialist period.

These indicators point-out to a very unequal distribution of world resources in science and technology that mimics also large disparities in per capita income across nations. Rich countries spend more in science in technology than middle income and poor countries. However, there are some significant outliers such as China and India whose ratios of spending in science and technology to GDP are significantly higher than the international average corresponding to their income per capita levels.

As already mentioned high skill and talented people leave their home countries for a variety of reasons: the possibility of acquiring knowledge and first rate education in the best centers of the world (education phase), the lure of interacting with peers of international recognition, the aim of pursuing a successful career abroad. Intellectual creation is rarely a purely individual endeavor: interactions with peers is a critical ingredient of the creative process. Human capital depends, positively, on the availability of human capital, in other words there are increasing returns in knowledge creation. In the decision to emigrate physicists seek other physicists, biologists seek other biologists, economists seek other economists, etc.

Matching, complementarities and increasing returns are thus an essential part of the story of emigration of human capital. As the literature on growth and development emphasises this can lead to virtuous circles and also to poverty traps. Receiving countries can set in motion a cycle of vigorous knowledge creation and application by attracting the most talented from abroad, who combine with an often strong knowledge base in the host country.

Conversely, sending countries can enter in a phase of stagnation in the development of science, technology and knowledge following the outflows of talent as a critical mass of scientists and technical experts disappear, deteriorating the milieu for knowledge generation and assimilation at home.

### *Human Capital Emigration-return Cycle*

The possibility of virtuous cycles of knowledge creation along with "knowledge traps" associated with the international mobility of human capital depend also on the nature of the emigration-return process. The foreign student chooses to remain abroad after completing higher education. The duration of the stay abroad can range from a few years, a decade to eventual retirement. If after a few years of work abroad the individual returns home, the emigration of human capital can be understood more as a "brain cycle" and not an irreversible loss.

In the case that the emigrant decides to stay abroad during his whole productive life the loss for the sending country is larger and the situation resembles more the "brain drain" symptom. In a world of lower transport costs and easy communications the talented individual living abroad may maintain contact and professional exchange with its peers at home, including periodic visits to his native country thus contributing (indirectly or directly) to national development in his or her area of expertise.

A main purpose of these networks is to connect professionals and scientists scattered around the globe who are interested in maintaining contact among themselves. In addition, they are also interested in helping to promote the scientific and economic development of their home countries. These networks may have a link with national governments or be fully independent. Scientific knowledge generation taking place in the world to networks, in principle, de-link the contribution of scientists to their physical residence in the home country and thus can be in interesting vehicle for transferring developing countries.

An important feature of migration, relatively neglected in the discussions of brain drain, is the international mobility of entrepreneurship. This is people that settle in other countries- developed and developing-and have a talent for business creation and job generation. There is considerable variation in the scale of the business activity created by the entreprenuership of foreign migrants. There is, indeed, a plethora of them operating at the level of family business and small firms. A typical example is the ethnic restaurants in the large cities of the developed countries.

This pattern of immigrant entrepreneurship do not mobilise large amounts of financial resources but they can be quite labor intensive and their business add to services variety in the host countries. The sociological profile of these endeavors is interesting: business are usually owned and run by members of a specific ethnic group and the employees (many times family members) tend to be also of the same ethnicity. The connections between ethnicity, entrepreneurship and migration and their patterns of integration/exclusion with the local economy and society are themes that deserve further inquire.

The relationship between endowments of human capital and entrepreneurship is also an interesting subject. Entrepreneurs are not necessarily people with a high stock of formal education; in addition, the " psychology of the entrepreneur" is certainly different from that of the scientist or the intellectual who we usually identify with "human capital". Typically the entrepreneur is prone to risk-taking, has a talent for combining capital, labor and for entertaining a vision of opportunities and the prospects for profits. In contrast, professionals, scientists engineers are often employees rather than owners and are supposed to be more risk averse.

In a world without barriers to the movement of people across nations, individuals should be expected to migrate from places where their productivity (and income) is lower to places where their productivity is higher, regardless of national borders. Then, human capital will go from lower net returns to higher net return places discounted the costs of moving (including some psychological costs of leaving home). Unless there are some significant negative externalities, "world income" should be higher with more mobile human capital as at the margin the marginal productivity of human capital will be equalised around the world. This, however, does not consider the distributional impact of such migrations flows between sending and receiving nations.

We live in a world of large disparities in levels of per capita income across countries and the movement of human capital from low income countries to rich nations may tend to accentuate these income per capita differentials. In fact, the emigration of the highly skilled increases the stock of human capital in advanced receiving countries and reduces it in lower per capita income (sending) countries. If, as mentioned before, there are increasing returns in human capital and it tends to concentrate in places where the availability of human and physical capital is already high the result may be an unequalising process of income and knowledge concentration across countries that tend to be persistent over time.

Under increasing returns, the international mobility of talent and human capital from poor to rich countries may exacerbate global inequalities. The impact of the outflows of human capital on national development of the sending countries can be negative in the short run as these outflows deprive the home country of their contribution to science, productivity and ultimately domestic output, reduce a source of revenues and weakens the middle class. In the medium and long runs things can improve.

To recognise that legal impediments for international migration of human capital and/or stiff taxation of those flows are unlikely to succeed and can be ultimately counterproductive. Those measures are likely to stifle individual preferences for mobility and dampen the motivation of scientists, technical experts and other skilled individuals. In the era of globalisation and rapid technical change the international mobility of human capital is unavoidable. The crucial point is how to create better economic and professional conditions for the high skilled and talented to return home, after studying or working abroad.

This reflects the existence of other priorities for resource allocation such as physical infrastructure and social spending over the development of science and technology. In the medium to long run, the neglect on the science and technology sector is likely to be reflected in lower productivity growth and competitiveness, hampering the development potential of these countries.

There is a role also for foreign aid in the area of science and technology to developing countries. Foreign aid in S&T can take several forms: support for universities and high-quality research centers in LDCs to enhance research capabilities and induce the repatriation of scientists and professionals. Another mechanism is creating programs of international exchange of scientists in which technical experts of developed countries can spend time in developing countries interacting with local researchers, thus contributing to the local development of the science and technology sector.

The use of the internet and support for local libraries in upgrading their collections of books, data bases, specialised journals and the like are concrete measures to help in this area. This aid can be channeled bilaterally or through international organisations such as UNESCO, The World Bank, OECD and others. Currently, the World Bank has a lending program for supporting the development of science in LDCs through the Millenium Science Initiative (MSI).

The loans go to national governments that provide matching funds and give financial support - often through grants- to the formation and maintenance of "centers of excellence" in science in their countries.

## Social Protection

The current growth in interest in development agencies in the issue of social protection derives, to a large extent, from the global reaction to various forms of economic or financial crisis over the 1990s. These have been seen to be associated with contemporary processes of globalisation, and specifically with the growing integration of trade systems and capital markets, which are generally seen to present two contrasting faces.

On the one hand, they are seen as increasing opportunities for all, while on the other hand they are seen as increasing insecurity on a global scale. Other dimensions of contemporary global change of relevance include:

- *Increasing inequality*: both within countries and between countries;
- An increasingly liberalised international economic environment restricting many sources of revenue which were previously available to governments to fund social expenditures; and
- A global demographic transition which implies long-term changes in dependency ratios (in particular, the growth in the absolute and relative numerical importance of older people).

In short, processes of international economic integration are increasingly leaving nation states with less power to regulate conditions for relationships between capital and labour, conditions of access to internal markets, and levels of budgetary support available for human development.

Development processes are also contributing to positive processes of human development which may enhance pressures on public resources in the field of social protection. Yet processes of accelerated integration of global societies and economies - which have great potential for increasing growth and human well-being - may in the long run be threatened if growing inequality leads to a perception that basic requirements of social justice are not being met. Analysis suggests that the institutional framework for social policy must adapt in response, at the local, national and global levels - although the appropriate agenda for such a response is still contested.

Rights to elements of social protection are contained in the Universal Declaration of Human Rights. In order to make these rights meaningful at the national level, governments and the international community need to meet the following challenges. Notions of social protection need to be converted into entitlements and standards which embody a sufficient level of consensus about the state's role, and the levels of risk and deprivation that are unacceptable within a given society, to ensure policy which is deliverable, effective and sustainable. In the literature on social protection in general the dimensions of governance and rights seem underdeveloped.

Diversity of definitions of and approaches to social protection which are adopted by international development agencies as they develop policy in this field. The first issue that needs to be addressed is the distinction, if any, between social protection and alternative terms in circulation. Social security is the most long-established of these terms. However, it is still primarily associated with the comprehensive and sophisticated social insurance and social assistance machinery of the developed world. As such, it is seen by some as inappropriate to the debate in much of the developing world, where higher levels of absolute poverty, combined with financially and institutionally weak states, pose a set of fundamentally different challenges.

The more recent terminology of safety nets (or sometimes more specifically social safety nets) is by contrast associated primarily with developing countries. These terms imply a more limited range of interventions - notably targeted social assistance (often now administered through social funds) - which have often been originally conceived as short-term, compensatory measures during structural adjustment or other national crises. Social protection has only come into widespread use relatively recently.

However, there is also a danger that different academics and development agencies use social protection with different definitions in mind.

Understandings of the meaning of social protection vary in a number of ways - between broad and narrow perspectives; between definitions which focus on the nature of the deprivations and problems addressed, and those which focus on the policy instruments used to address them; and between those which take a conceptual as opposed to a pragmatic approach to the task. Most definitions have a dual character, referring to both the nature of deprivation and the form of policy response.

Social protection deals with both the absolute deprivation and vulnerabilities of the poorest, and also with the need of the non-poor for security in the face of shocks and the particular demands of different stages of the life-cycle. As such, it encompasses as its core the two main broad fields of response mechanism, namely social assistance and social insurance..

Social assistance is defined as benefits in cash or in kinds that are financed by the state (national or local) and that are mostly provided on the basis of a means or income text. The concept also includes universal benefit schemes, i.e. those which are taxbased but do not use a means test. Social insurance is social security that is financed by contributions and is based on the insurance principle.

The essence of insurance is understood here to be the elimination of the uncertain risk of loss for the individual or household by combining a larger number of similarly exposed individuals or households into a common fund that makes good the loss caused to any one member. This description is not specific regarding the identity of the institutions providing insurance-based social protection, but identifies the state as provider of social assistance.

Given the importance of informal transfers in the livelihoods of the poor, and in keeping with a broad definition of social protection proposed above, the concept of social assistance should not be restricted to state funded transfers, but apply to all forms of public action which are designed to transfer resources to groups deemed eligible due to deprivation. This eligibility may be seen in terms of income poverty, or in terms of other dimensions of deprivation.

Similarly, insurance is understood broadly to encompass any form of pooling of resources among groups to provide protection against risk. Insurance schemes may be state-run, state-regulated but run in the private sector, or informal. Response to risk and deprivation may take the form of strengthening collective, membership-based responses to risk; statutory instruments which enhance security; interventions which enhance access to employment and secure tenure of assets; and direct interventions to ensure minimum acceptable standards of livelihood for those with insufficient assets to secure a livelihood.

The field of social protection thus encompasses many different areas and traditions of policy response. Many of these are highly technical and specialised in character. The linkage between social protection and broader social policy analysis is important to the analysis and prioritisation of public expenditures and public policy choices. Particularly in poorer countries, difficult choices need to be made in relation to the capacity of the state and the need to direct financial, institutional and human resources at different fields, including for example health, education and water as well as social protection.

Secondly, it is important not to see social protection as a field that deals only with residual problems of human welfare, but as a form of policy which liberates human potential and promotes equality of opportunity as well as of outcome. It is possible to see a balanced approach to social protection contributing to economic well-being through three channe

- by increasing security, through helping households and communities sustain their livelihoods in the face of economic, political, environmental, health or other shocks - as well as reducing the likelihood of such shocks occurring;
- by contributing to equality through
  - promoting levels of livelihood sufficient to ensure enhanced equality of opportunity by allowing for all households to achieve basic education for their children, as well as standards of health and nutrition necessary for human development, and
  - raising the levels of consumption and livelihood of the poorest; and
- by promoting growth through:
  - ensuring that all households have the wherewithal to provide for basic human development thus ensuring a skilled, productive workforce,
  - reinforcing values of social solidarity and thereby contributing to levels of social cohesion necessary for long-term economic development, and
  - providing an environment in which individuals and households are able to adapt and change livelihood strategies without fear of calamity should such strategies fail.

The use of statutory forms of social insurance for providing pensions and other benefits to workers in uneconomic state enterprises for example, has been shown in practice to enhance inequality in many developing countries, by effectively taxing poorer workers to provide benefits for the nonpoor. There is also the obvious danger that a growing burden of public expenditure in social assistance transfers may destabilise the public budget and undermine the capacity to provide the core investments in public infrastructure and services that a country needs for growth and security of livelihoods.

## Rationale for Social Protection

*The case for the systematic treatment of social protection*: The rationale for involving government in social protection, rather than leaving action to the private sector, relates to the inability of the private sector unaided to solve two problems: firstly the low level of income (and hence high poverty) of some individuals or groups, and secondly the vulnerability of others to transient poverty due to high variability of incomes and lack of effective consumption smoothing strategies.

Transient poverty can become permanent if, for example, indebtedness or sales of assets reduce future income earning potential. On the first point regarding low average living standards, market mechanisms, however well they function, do not guarantee a minimally acceptable standard of life if individuals or groups have insufficient assets. Transfers of assets or income are needed to deal with the moral obligation to guarantee this minimum standard. Regarding the second point of variability, insurance markets are notoriously incomplete for well understood reasons of market failure: inadequate information with which to assess risk, adverse selection, moral hazard, high transactions costs for poor and dispersed populations, and covariant risks.

The problem of absolute average poverty requires redistributive policies. These can be of three main types:

- Increasing the level and range of assets available to the poorest (e.g. land reform, investments in human capital through health and education, or physical capital to raise the returns to the assets they have). These interventions would be indistinguishable from general poverty reduction policies. Though primarily aimed at raising average income, asset transfers also enable poor people to smooth consumption more effectively because they can diversify income sources, and sell or mortgage assets when bad times strike.

- Measures to raise the returns on assets held by the poor, for example by raising the demand for their labour through employment schemes, or to raise wages or the price of crops produced by the poor.
- Direct targeted transfers of income, in cash or in kind. These can take the form of direct financial transfers, or transfers in kind through free or subsidised access to merit goods e.g. food rations at free or subsidised prices, or exemptions from user fees. The central problem is how to target the poor while minimising leakage to the non-poor, keeping costs manageable, and avoiding incentive problems and the creation of dependence.

The insurance role of the state in smoothing consumption can occur at a range of levels from macro to micro. All governments have a responsibility to react to emergency situations affecting large numbers of people. For shocks which are widespread in scope, the state holds foreign exchange reserves which can be converted to extra spending to meet needs at short notice. The state may also hold emergency food grain reserves.

Governments are also able to borrow and to call on the donor community in dealing with widespread emergencies. There are linkages between contingency planning for such events and ongoing social protection provision. Where an administrative infrastructure exists for providing targeted support to the poorest, for example through food for work and other feeding schemes, it can more readily be expanded in times of emergency.

The extent to which the state can practically intervene to protect individuals from misfortune is in practice very much more limited in low-income countries. Where many are poor, difficult choices have to be made about the resources devoted to the poorest of the poor, with potential trade-offs between development activities and state funded forms of social protection. Although there may be the opportunity for beneficial public sector intervention, there are also opportunity costs.

In looking at which measures a government can afford and can practically implement, affordability, capacity and accountability of government action will be key considerations. The late 1990s showed a growing concern with the global dimensions of social policy, evident in both the academic literature and policy developments. Perhaps the defining event of this period, the event which provoked the international community to examine the changing environment for economic and social policy and its relationship to the institutional framework for managing risk and promoting opportunity, was the Asian financial crisis that broke in mid-1997.

This crisis resulted in serious economic recession and hardship in countries which had previously been regarded as developmental success stories. Although policy regimes obviously differed considerably between the countries affected, they could all be characterised as having pursued a relatively open, growth-led path to development and poverty reduction. This general strategy of rapid, broad-based economic growth had been widely praised and, albeit with different interpretations and emphases, recommended as a suitable development strategy in international policy discourse.

Arguably, however, the neglect of social protection mechanisms made these countries vulnerable, following an economic crash, to rapid increases in poverty and the adoption of household-level coping mechanisms which slowed economic recovery and undermined long-term human development. These vulnerabilities were only really exposed from 1997, when economic recession hit harder than it would have done had such policies and programmes been in place. Governments, academics and multilateral institutions are now debating the proposition that new global institutional arrangements are needed in a world of increased economic volatility, and are examining the implications of such change for economic and social policy.

These events clearly form part of the ongoing debates concerning the various phenomena described under the term 'globalisation'. Globalisation is taken as having two key aspects: firstly, accelerated global integration of various kinds and, secondly, the institutional responses to these integrative processes, occurring at various levels, from global through regional and national to local scales.

Particularly in the aftermath of the Asian crisis, analysis of the economic and social consequences of globalisation tends to stress two differing and parallel dimensions. On the one hand, current global processes of change are seen as increasing opportunities for all, including poorer people and poorer countries. On the other hand, they are seen as exacerbating insecurity on a global scale, in terms of both the increased probability that economic shocks will be international rather than national in scale, and the increased severity of those shocks when they do occur.

The increasing focus on social protection in international development organisations can thus be seen, at least in part, as the reactions of policy-makers to the various financial crises of the 1990s. Underlying this has been the general trend towards re-focussing development co-operation on the elimination of poverty. Much of this policy-focussed analysis has concentrated upon addressing national and sub-national processes that cause or reduce poverty. Increasingly, however, the anti-poverty debate has also addressed distinctive features of contemporary globalisation which are seen to necessitate a policy response at the supra-national level.

In response to these trends the ILO advocates increased international attention to action in four areas: education and training; social safety nets; labour law and industrial relations; and core labour standards. Improved social protection is therefore seen as one of four pillars of socially responsive globalisation, fulfilling two 'complementary purposes': the equitable distribution of the costs and benefits of globalisation and restructuring; and the strengthening of societal support for reform processes.

There is a danger that processes of international economic integration are increasingly leaving nation states - and poorer nation states in particular - with less power to regulate conditions for relationships between capital and labour, conditions of access to internal markets, and the levels of budgetary support available for human development. As the nation state remains the major framework for systems of formal political participation there is a clear danger of a vacuum developing in terms of authority and accountability as this process extends.

Processes of accelerated integration of global societies and economies - processes which have great potential for increasing growth and human well-being - may in the long run be threatened if growing inequality leads to a perception that basic standards of social justice are not being met. This analysis suggests that the institutional framework for social policy must adapt in response, at the local, national and global levels. The appropriate agenda for such a response is, however, still contested.

Drawing on recent thinking on social policy in the North, it is important to register that social policy is inextricably linked to economic policy, and not a residual category of public policy dealing with welfare. Good social policy is increasingly needed to provide the investment needed for a cohesive, dynamic society with a skilled and healthy workforce. In short, it is as much about enhancing opportunities as it is about providing protection for those not able to find a sufficient livelihood through the market or institutions of kinship and community. Another significant process of global change is the ongoing global demographic transition from high birth and death rates to low.

This transition implies long-term growth in the absolute numbers and relative proportions of older people. Improvements in medical care and reproductive health are leading to longer life spans and posing a complex global challenge to systems of social protection for older people. This problem will underscore the need to find means of social protection which are flexible, cost-effective, and make the most use of the active capabilities of groups often stereotyped as unable to be active contributors to society and development.

***Literature on Poverty and Deprivation***

The increasing importance attached to social protection issues within debates upon poverty reduction can be illustrated by comparing the two 'decennial' World Bank World Development Reports which deal with the theme of poverty. The inclusion of this theme was a landmark in re-focusing attention on the social protection role of the state in the aftermath of the neo-liberal consensus of the 1980s. Much of the debate during the 1990s was critical of the 'safety net' formulation, however, which implied a perception of the poorest as passive recipients of transfers rather than as active agents.

The literature on risk and vulnerability falls broadly within two traditions. One is based on participatory and ethnographic understandings of the nature of poor people's realities and livelihoods. This material has been influential in bringing issues of vulnerability into the mainstream of policy debate. In the late 1980s and early 1990s when quantitative survey based approaches focused on providing static 'snapshot' pictures of the levels of deprivation, this literature emphasised the fact that poor people's own perceptions of well being placed considerable emphasis on issues of security, both of the person and of livelihoods.

The other tradition comprises a comprehensive re-visiting of the issue of risk and vulnerability in empirical, quantitative, and conceptual economic analysis. This is a rich literature that encompasses most recent developments and trends in the analysis of poverty and deprivation. Both traditions emphasise the importance of analysing vulnerability from the perspectives of endowments of assets that can be accessed by poor households, individuals or communities.

These assets are not simply material - the analytical framework of 'sustainable rural livelihoods', for example, groups assets into five types of capital (physical, natural, financial, social and human). The literature also shows how assets are significant not simply as aids to production but also as stores of wealth, buffering individuals and households against hard times. This goes for social capital as much as it does for physical capital: social networks that can be used to increase wellbeing also enable people to make claims on others in times of trouble.

The idea that forms of mutual insurance which protect against risk and eventualities such as old age are fundamental to the mutual solidarity that underpins society is not new. Principles of reciprocity and mutual obligation are fundamental to the values of solidarity and identity that underpin the cohesion of societies.

In its original form social exclusion refers primarily to a rupture of the social and moral bonds between an individual or group and society. There is not the space here to discuss at length the linkages between social protection policy and the rich theoretical tradition concerning social exclusion in developed and developing countries. Civil society activism in the North is steadily moving in emphasis from charitable giving to addressing structural issues of social justice. These shifts constitute encouraging evidence of the growth of new forms of global solidarity, although the capacity to address growing polarisation within the global economy clearly has limits.

***Political Dimensions, Rights and Accountability***

There is a growing literature suggesting linkages between the nature of national governance and the effective reduction of poverty. A cross-country study of 61 developing countries30 found that the effectiveness of a country at converting resources into human development was correlated with the extent to which the state was dependent on its citizens for revenue, rather than upon extractive industries or donors. This suggests that the accountability of public services delivery tends to be reinforced (at least under some conditions) through dependence upon a broad revenue base.

Historical studies of the development of welfare capacities in both developed and developing countries suggest that the level of livelihood risk is a key determinant of the level of state interventions with social objectives. This is because many poor countries lack the capacity to implement effective social welfare programmes to mitigate risk, so substitute for this by creating government jobs and 'development programmes' which have reach key constituencies of political support, if not the broader population.

The policy implications thus point strongly to the critical need in most developing country contexts to strengthen capacities at an institutional level, and the structure of governance and accountability. The lack of entitlement to state social protection has deep roots in many developing countries. While race is no longer the principle dimension of exclusion, the legacy of the bifurcated society persists. It underpins the current division in many Africa states between 'citizens' who work in the core segments of the labour market and enjoy decent wages, job security and working conditions as well as social benefits, and 'subjects' who occupy the marginalised, often rural segments which are characterised by informal livelihoods and low levels of access to public provisioning and services.

This type of segmentation has major policy implications for social protection, which can be addressed through technocratic programme design. It has to be recognised, however, that in full-blown form structural inequalities of this kind are problematic not just for the detail of programme design, but for the development of governance and society at a fundamental level.

## Development Agency on Social Protection

*Influences upon agency position regarding social policy*: The first point to note is that development agencies bring with them to the issue of social protection a set of concerns, some which are reasonably general and some of which are variable.

Most donor agencies see their role as supporting long-term reductions in poverty, which offers an eventual reduction in the need for aid, rather than providing protection of livelihoods, especially where such assistance has characteristics of a recurrent service with no clear exit. But the increasing recognition of the necessity for development agencies to engage with the full range of governmental policies in partner countries, and to take a long-term view of the development process, implies a certain convergence of interest.

As social protection expenditures form part of a country's overall budget and social policy actions, even agencies which do not specialise historically in that area will be forced to develop understanding in the field.

*Current directions in agency policy*: The ADB has relatively recently adopted as its overarching mission 'to help its developing members achieve accelerated and irreversible reductions in poverty'. Social protection is seen as an integral component of this goal. Interestingly, this contribution to poverty reduction is presented in terms of social protection 'making growth more efficient and equitable', through smoothing the functioning of labour markets, facilitating investment in human capital, and providing the poor with the subsistence security which will enable them to take productive risks.

This presentation of the rationale for ADB work in social protection thus resembles that in the World Bank. The follow-through - in terms of identification of country-level influences upon social protection development strategies and elaboration of implications for ADB operations - is pragmatic and flexible. Given the specific challenges of Asia, broad-based demographic structures, the largest numbers of poor people in the world and a large informal sector, specific attention is given to labour market policies, crop insurance and price supports for agriculture, social assistance and welfare.

The one notable and explicit exclusion from its definition of social protection is health insurance, on the grounds that this is best considered in context of other health sector policies relating to the delivery of health care.

***International Labour Office***

The ILO approach to social security is, as mentioned above, in the late stages of a period of transition. Traditionally, the ILO has sought to promote the development of statutory social insurance programmes along a model based upon the historical experience of the developed world. While there is some division of responsibility for social protection work between different units within the organisation, it seems fair to say that in the 1990s the emphasis has shifted, with new conceptual work concentrating primarily upon the development of a range of appropriate forms of insurance-based social protection for the informal sector.

The starting point for the current ILO strategy is the observation that only a very small proportion of the population of the developing world enjoys any protection from conventional statutory social security instruments. Pilot studies in India, Tanzania, El Salvador and Benin in the second half of the 1990s have examined the reasons for this poor coverage; drawn out the general patterns in what the social protection priorities of the poor actually are; and identified the possibilities for encompassing those presently excluded, whether by extending statutory systems or developing alternatives to these systems.

Analysis of the strengths and weaknesses of innovative schemes in these countries has provided insights into the possibilities for extending social insurance to the informal sector. Incorporating domestic work and the 'care economy', this approach is distinguished by four specific features: an emphasis upon universality of coverage and pervasiveness of concern; the use of the idea of rights; the conceptual location of work conditions within a broad economic, social and political context that stresses democracy and participation; and the search for global rather than merely international policies.

The most operationally-developed elements of the ILO's current social protection approach nonetheless still reflects its focus upon employment issues in its primary focus upon insurancebased mechanisms. Perhaps surprisingly, the new work in the ILO seems to pay relatively little attention to employment generation / public works schemes, which despite their problems remain a popular approach to social protection in many countries.

### *World Bank*

The World Bank is increasingly influential in the development of social protection approaches. The Bank's lending in social protection activities has grown rapidly over the 1990s. The Social Protection Sector was established in 1996, drawing on and, gradually, drawing together various traditions of social protection work within the Bank. Through 1999 Sector staff in the Bank worked to develop a cohesive conceptual basis for these diverse approaches to social protection.

The major part of the theoretical treatment focuses upon how policy can help the poor to manage risk in the interest of human capital development and the prudent risk-taking necessary for long-term, poverty-reducing economic growth. The focus on qualitative and experiential dimensions of poverty is striking in WDR 2000, in which the theme of 'security' is developed as one of three central components required for a sustainable poverty reduction strategy.

The strengths of the Bank's contribution can be seen to lie in its growing experience with different approaches to social protection, the influence it can bring to bear by virtue of the volume of lending activities in this sector, and the considerable volume of conceptual work on risk and risk management produced in the last two years. It should be noted that the increasing involvement of IFIs in the social policy domain is not always welcomed. Some developing countries fear that this involvement will eventually lead to loan conditionality based on inappropriate standards of social policy.

Social protection policy have placed started to place more emphasis upon understanding social protection mechanisms provided by non-state institutions. These institutions include family and kin, 'community', religious bodies, non-governmental organisations, savings and credit groups, and forms of 'traditional' insurance such as burial societies. There are collective arrangements which provide both forms of insurance against various kinds of risk through pooling of resources, and assistance to the long-term poor and people in situations of temporary crisis.

However, we do not know enough about the effectiveness and resilience of these institutions, or their policy significance. In particular, there has been a notable failure to translate the large and culturally particularistic sociological literature on coping and survival strategies into adequate general principles for policy makers.

*Social protection, patronage and 'community'*: The literature on socially-based risk reduction, mitigation and coping strategies is large. Much of it draws upon the concept of the 'moral economy' in traditional societies with small and relatively weak states. This literature on moral economies encompasses several concepts. The first concept is that the poor - often constituting the majority in a society - live so close to the subsistence threshold that even a small shock will push them into a survival crisis.

Household strategies for groups in this situation therefore focus upon minimising risk. These strategies to minimise the probability of risk generally come with a trade-off. They may make the consequences of crisis more severe when it can't be avoided. Perhaps even more importantly, strategies which serve to reduce risk in the short to medium term may actually make it harder to make the transition to a low risk environment in the long term. There are numerous examples of this 'perverse' trade-off between poverty and security.

Risk minimisation and mitigation strategies are, for example, often achieved through seeking patrons: in this 'lop-sided friendship,' the poor may accept routine exploitation which keeps them in poverty in return for the promise of protection when crisis does strike. Similarly, the risk-minimisation strategies of the poor often entail choosing low return options over potentially high-return options. The result is that the poor remain trapped in poverty, accepting exploitation and / or settling for low productivity in return for some minimal livelihood security; unable to take risks because any failure would be disastrous, they are unable to attempt high return activities which would allow them to diversify their livelihood base or acquire assets and savings.

More recently, reflecting the efforts of sociologists to deconstruct the household, emphasis has been placed upon the intra-household arrangements which in many ways mirror the 'safety-first' principles observed in inter-household ('community') relationships. In many societies women settle for unequal and exploitative relationships to their husbands because these relationships also entail some reciprocal responsibilities and protection - at least in theory (cultural ideal), if not always in reality (cultural practice).

*Social protection and common property*: It has been noted that access to common property resources (CPRs) is a crucial element of the livelihood strategies of the poor in rural societies. Fish from rivers and lakes, timber and nontimber products from forests, and field crops such as frogs, crabs and birds may all be essential to the consumption and income of rural households. Common property resources are particularly important as a fall-back strategy in times of trouble.

For this reason, social conventions regarding who does and does not have access to the commons are often fiercely defended. Economic, demographic or legal transformations which infringe upon customary rights to these resources can have seriously regressive effects upon the poor. The consequences of the erosion of common property rights is often gradual and attracts little attention until a crisis, when shocks which were previously serious become catastrophic. The significance of common property resources for poor people is considerably exaggerated in situations of widespread rural landlessness.

It is thus worth simply noting from a policy perspective that access to common property is a key area for an integrated policy of social protection, especially in relation to rural areas. Under some conditions the access of poor people to CPRs may be contested - and involve negotiations with the state, as in the case of forest reserves, wildlife parks and often with rivers and lakes. If sustainable forms of resource management can be developed which allow the poor legitimate access without harassment, the potential benefits are often very significant. Institutions which promote such sustainable management are important elements of the context for sustainable social protection at the community level.

*Religious organisation and social protection*: In many societies organised religion provided and in some cases still provides refuge of last resort to the completely destitute. In some societies religious conversion can be interpreted as (amongst other things) an effort to escape ascribed social identities (e.g. caste) which confine their members to impoverished, high-risk lives.

More directly, changing religion may allow the convert to claim the support of the new church. In situations of widespread distress religious groups also frequently provide a 'bridge' between the local environment and external sources of support. Such structures may of course deliver benefits in an exclusionary fashion - although this is by no means always the case.

*Community Based Organisations and NGOs*: The widespread involvement of various forms of developmental and charitable organisation (local, national and international) is of obvious relevance to the discussion of social protection. Local and international NGOs generally operate with a strong value-based motivation, many concentrating on assistance to the poorest.

The basic principles of a functioning social protection system are that it should provide appropriate and effective means of alleviating absolute deprivation and protecting against the risk of a decline in livelihoods. It should start with the poorest, and be achieved through arrangements which are socially and politically acceptable and financially sustainable. These ends may be achieved through a variety of instruments and institutional arrangements. This perspective has been adopted in recognition of the low institutional and financial capacity of the state in most developing countries to engage heavily in direct transfers to the poor.

### *Labour Market Policies*

In the long term, the primary route to individual and household security for the vast majority of the urban poor, and many of the rural poor in developing countries, is through income obtained via wage employment. Labour market policies are intended to facilitate the operation of labour markets in the interests of fuller and more financially rewarding employment. Major components include:

— *The adoption of labour standards*: These are of two kinds. The so-called 'core-labour standards' agenda has become widely accepted as part of the fabric of economic and social rights to which the global community aspires. More detailed provisions which protect specific material aspects of working conditions can provide workers in the formal sector with good incomes, but may limit the growth and flexibility of formal sector employment, and exacerbate the gaps between the standards which apply in the formal sector, and much worse conditions in the much larger, unregulated informal sector.

  Legislation which makes it more difficult and costly for employers to shed labour have a particularly negative impact on recruitment. This is one aspect of social protection policy in which global principles are likely to be an important influence. The challenge for policy makers is to engage in an equitable fashion with the realities of employment - and seek to strengthen rights and standards for everyone within the economy, rather than privileging specific groups.

- Active labour market interventions which smooth supply and demand in labour markets, matching workers with appropriate employers. Labour exchanges help workers to find suitable vacancies; similar schemes can put workers in touch with training programmes to upgrade their skills.
- Packages of interventions to absorb some of the shock of major restructuring. These may include retraining, assistance with placements and contributions towards migration costs.
- Legislation against discriminatory practices which exclude women or particular ethnic groups, or result in low pay for these groups.

In the rich world, much of the statutory social protection machinery takes the form of social insurance, that is, social security financed by contributions from the beneficiaries and based upon the insurance principle. A large number of individuals or households which have roughly equal social protection needs combine to mitigate risks, pooling their contributions in a common fund which can then provide pre-defined benefits to members in the event of specified occurrences.

Under many statutory schemes the contribution from the employee is matched by an obligatory contribution from the employer and / or the state. The risks covered can be related to a fall in income or to an unexpected rise in expenditure. The extent to which statutory social insurance operates as a genuine insurance fund varies. In many poor countries strapped for cash, social insurance schemes have been either raided to pay for general public expenditures, or have been obliged to invest in low yielding investments in for example nationalised industries, or poorly remunerated state borrowing.

The nature of the implicit insurance 'contract' can also be problematic. If the government is free to influence the terms of what is provided, or if poor investment policies are combined with domestic inflation, the insurance actually provided can be of very limited value. Employment-based social insurance schemes typically provide coverage against unemployment, inability to work due to injury or ill health, and, ultimately, old age. Contributions assure a continued income stream in the event of not being able to work. Particularly with regard to pensions, this replacement income may be fixed or earnings-related.

The problem is that in most low-income countries the majority of the workforce is not involved in permanent wage labour in the formal sector. Workers in the informal sector are not effectively involved in statutory social insurance schemes, for several reasons.

- Firstly, premiums are beyond the financial reach of most of the poor. The problem is not only that total contribution requirements are too high, but that they do not take account of the variable income patterns of the poor. Contributory insurance schemes are generally premised upon the principle of a pre-defined benefit in the event of a specified crisis, regardless of the length of time over which contributions have been made or the total individual contribution that has accumulated. Eligibility through continuous, regular contributions is most effectively ensured by deducting social insurance contributions from wages at source.

  The employer's contribution is collected in the same way. Workers in the informal sector, particularly casual labourers who work for short periods with many different employers, often in many different places, find it hard to maintain a consistent record of contribution.

- Most social insurance is based upon the principle of a 'replacement wage', with benefits paid at a set proportion of the income lost due to inability to work. It is hard to define what the replacement wage should be for informal sector workers, particularly casual labourers, given the great variability in wages from one week or month to the next. The valuation of nonmonetary income - food produced for on-farm consumption, or wages paid in kind - also make it hard to determine what constitutes a replacement wage.

- Informal sector employers are generally outside the web of routine state surveillance and regulation. They are generally not registered, have few capital assets, employ workers at below the legal minimum wage without written contracts, do not keep precise accounts, and do not pay taxes. It can be very hard to obtain a fixed, regular employer's contribution from such enterprises, or even to arrange for them to collect employees' contributions through the payroll.

  There are several ways in which states might attempt to extend social insurance to the informalsector majority who currently enjoy little if any such protection. The coverage of existing social insurance schemes can be extended somewhat by removing legal restrictions upon scheme membership, and by streamlining administrative structures and procedures. Pension schemes may benefit from re-appraising the balance between the risks and opportunities associated with pay-as-you-go (PAYG) financing as compared to 'funded' financing.

  The ILO recommends that 'pay as you go' is more appropriate for mandatory systems providing minimum and some earnings-related pensions, while the 'funded' approach is better suited for voluntary and some mandatory schemes providing earnings-related pensions.

More ambitiously, states could complement conventional schemes with schemes which provide either

- benefits proportionate to the contributions that have been made or

– fixed benefits once a set amount has been contributed. Such systems are more suited to the irregular earning patterns of the informal sector: workers make contributions to their social insurance as and when they are able to, rather than providing a contribution of a set amount (or set proportion of a variable amount) on a regular basis.

These approaches, however, depend on building trust in government institutions. In many poor countries, then, the main method by which to extend social insurance coverage in the medium term is through the promotion of voluntary insurance associations. Within these associations, groups of informal sector workers pool contributions of an agreed size according to an appropriate schedule; agree the mechanism for collection and administration of funds; and define the size and conditions of benefit payouts.

These arrangements are dependent on the development of financial institutions which are conveniently located and able to offer sufficient returns to protect from inflation. As these arrangements grow and become formalised into organisations with defined memberships, rules and administrative committees, they may benefit from legislation and administrative support provided by the state.

The emergence of Beneficial or Friendly societies in Britain between the late eighteenth and late nineteenth centuries is a relevant case in point. Analysis of such schemes in the contemporary developing world has confirmed the importance of the two fundamental requirements for success, namely

– the existence of an association based on trust and
– an administration which is capable of collecting contributions and paying benefits. Size is also crucial: the wider the membership, the better the scheme is placed to absorb the impact of covariant shocks and a glut of claims.

6

# Education of Children

Interest in youth and education and learning has been growing worldwide. Escalating youth needs are the concern of everyone-families, school systems. Youth tend to be viewed as a problem and at the very heart of many of our most pressing social concerns. Drugs, violence, delinquency, and teen pregnancy are problems youth have come to be associated with worldwide. Analyses of the situation of youth almost everywhere point to growing alienation, a lack of a sense of identity and of future, and disconnection from families, school, communities, and the broader society. Parents from all social backgrounds and cultures echo dissatisfaction with the educational and social support structures available to their children.

According to many experts, the generation gap and ensuing conflict are stronger than ever before. School systems are having a hard time coping with adolescents and youth. Following the strong emphasis given primary education in the South in the 1980s and 1990s, secondary education emerges as the new challenge for many of these countries in the first decade of this century. According to evaluation data, problems of discipline and violence, school dropouts, and low learning achievement characterise secondary education worldwide.

Youth appear at the crossroads of many of the most important societal concerns of our time. Family disintegration, poverty, war, and armed conflicts have resulted in millions of street children and youth, refugees, and lack of proper adult protection and affection for youth in all social classes. Unemployment grows, becomes structural in many societies, and is particularly pronounced among youth. The rapid growth of AIDS has affected adolescent and youth development, impacting the very nature of relations between genders at an early age.

The world many youth live in, and most youth are exposed to through mass media, is a world of injustice, violence, corruption, individualism, materialism, and financial and sexual abuses, where almost anything can be bought and sold. Rising violence and crime are also youth issues. Distrust of politics and political parties, in elections and in overall civic participation, are widespread among youth growing up in different contexts and cultures as revealed by a number of studies and surveys in many parts of the world.

## Glibalisation in Knowledge Society

Globalisation has come with the requirement and promise of a "knowledge society" and a "knowledge-based economy." Lifelong learning has emerged as a need for all and an organising principle of both educational and social systems. This shift also requires that teaching and learning be viewed as two distinct aspects of education. Teaching (pedagogical methodologies, curricula, academic content, the knowledge and information conveyed by the instructor) has received much attention; while learning (if and how the student internalises and processes that information, whether the student can apply it to new situations and generalise it, and any changes that take place in the student's world view because of the new knowledge) has received less attention.

So the education process is not complete or effective, unless teaching is reflected in actual learning from the student's perspective. There are various modern interpretations of the concept of lifelong learning. For many educators, the lifelong learning paradigm confronts the challenge of accepting the school system as one (among other) learning systems, and the need to transform it to cope with its new role. For analysts, lifelong learning is strongly associated with distance education and modern information and communication technologies (ICTs), not only as a complement but also as a substitute for schooling. In any case, it is commonly accepted that lifelong learning and the requirements of the upcoming knowledge society imply a major shift in the conventional education and learning culture.

Contemporary literature and programmes related to youth education point to important similarities across regions, countries, and cultures. Such similarities can be attributed to several factors, among them:

- commonalities of education and learning institutions worldwide;
- common characteristics and realities of this particular generation of youth, as distinct from previous generations of youth (each generation exhibits specific characteristics because each generation lives during a different historical period);
- the role of development agencies particularly in the case of developing and transitional countries; and
- the internationalization of ideas and trends vis á vis education, learning, youth and development, in an increasingly globalized society.

In the framework of such global trends, there are also many regional and national differences. Policies and programmes dealing with the education of youth differ between countries in the North and in the South, but also among and within the major geographic regions.While much of the terminology may give the impression of a common language, there remain important cultural, political, and ideological differences in the understanding, emphases, and concrete applications of such concepts. Thus, concern with school achievement and academic competencies has become a worldwide concern, but the terms of such concern differ between North and South, and within each region.

For example, programmes dealing with drug abuse are much more widespread in the North than in the South. Europe and the United States have somewhat different approaches to what and how youth should be learning in schools. Mathematical skills appear as a main concern in the U.S., while multiculturalism and tolerance are at the center of many youth development programmes in transition (ex-communist) countries in Europe. Programmes for street children and vocational training for youth are particularly widespread in Latin America, while a focus on girls' education is a major trend in many countries in Africa and Asia. Concepts such as life skills, cultural identity, leadership, self-esteem, entrepreneurship, critical thinking, resilience, citizenship and citizenship building, volunteerism, and many others, have different meanings in different cultures.

Traditionally, the education of children and youth has involved an adult-centered approach. Educational provision has been centered on adult perceptions of young people's needs, which have then been translated into curriculum, teaching strategies, and spatial and time arrangements.Typically, children and youth learning needs are defined based on demands posed by the family, the community, and the larger society. Most of these demands focus on helping the child or young person to succeed through various life transitions-to adulthood, to building a family, to work. Little attention has been given to what youth themselves have to say.

Even when consultation is involved, young people's opinions are usually framed within the logic of needs rather than of wants. The weaknesses of this adult-centered and authoritarian approach have become increasingly apparent. As the case below shows, young people are demanding to have a voice and to participate. Past failures speak to the need to involve youth-not only for the sake of their valuable contributions and participation in society-but because their knowledge and perceptions are critical for successful policy and programme design and implementation.

Important changes are taking place in this regard. Authoritarianism is no longer the prevailing trend in both the family and school system. More democratic relationships are emerging at home and in the school system. There are more and more examples of youth participating in school governing boards, actively defining, together with school authorities, the codes and regulations of the school. Many youth and educational reform efforts are now working to enable and enhance dialogue between students and teachers, between children and parents, and/or between students, teachers, and parents.

The notion of young people as protagonists with valid voices and valuable contributions is increasingly being integrated into programmes around the world, governmental and non-governmental. New tensions and contradictions also are emerging as a result of these trends. Roles and issues of authority, discipline, autonomy, and liberty are being redefined. The tension between learning needs (as perceived by adults and by youth themselves) and learning wants, or between learning for the present and learning for the future, is being addressed in curriculum and pedagogical design.

Experimentation is being advised before "going to scale." It has become increasingly clear that the only way to address such tensions, and to define and promote the best possible educational approaches, will be by engaging youth in the process. Increased poverty and social exclusion are some of the downsides of the market economy and of globalisation. Half of the world's population is currently categorised as poor or surviving below the poverty line, on less than two dollars a day.

To address these harsh realities, "poverty alleviation" and "compensatory" social policies focused on "disadvantaged" groups (also termed "marginalised," "at risk," "vulnerable," or "in especially difficult circumstances") have been emphasised over the past few years. Diverse groupings and conditions are included under this category, including working children, street children, low academic achievers, dropouts and out-of-school youth, pregnant adolescents and youth, drug abusers, refugees, and ethnic minorities.

Poverty is the organising category that underlies and furthers many of these conditions. The focus on "poor/disadvantaged/at risk groups" responds to a social inclusion approach aimed at ensuring social equity and is thus valuable. However, a closer look at many such inclusion policies and programmes reveals negative underlying assumptions and repercussions. On one hand, such focus has contributed to identifying youth with disadvantaged youth and disadvantaged youth with "problem" youth. All these associations and generalisations have added to the negative image of youth in general, and of disadvantaged youth in particular.

The very term "disadvantaged" may not be the most appropriate. Is disadvantaged a term that should be applied to people whether referring to children, youth or adults-or rather to their conditions? Do "the disadvantaged" see and call themselves such? How are such individuals disadvantaged- in what ways, with respect to whom, and to what? Calling attention to the problems of youth who live on the margins of society has increased the public's negative perception of them. Likewise, calling youth themselves "disadvantaged," rather than their situation, may have enhanced the negative image that society holds of them.

Such a focus obscures the needs and wants of youth as a generation, regardless of their family income, social status, or personal condition. In fact, as highlighted in abundant literature today, a crisis of identity, lack of sense of future, alienation, violent hehaviours, use of drugs, and difficulties securing satisfying jobs, affect both rich and poor all over the planet. Children and youth of all social strata are exposed to a globalised culture of individualism, materialism, violence, family disintegration, uncertainty, and loss of fundamental values. Effective policies and programmes should avoid reverse discrimination.

Rather than isolating specific youth groups in institutions and programmes addressed to them only, such policies adopt area-based, community-based, and whole-school approaches in order to promote interaction with other groups-indigenous children interacting with nonindigenous children, girls interacting with boys, the poor with the non-poor. Proyecto Axé, which works with street children, is a good example of this. Striving for maximum quality, and to combine formal and non-formal education, it decided to create a special school that is special not because it is "a school for street children" but a quality school that integrates all children from the neighborhood.

## Relation Between School and Community

Traditionally the linkages between school and community, and even between school and parents, have been weak and remain a key challenge to educational reform throughout the world. Emphasis has tended to be, and remains, on internal dynamics within schools and not on external forces in a young person's life. Research and experience have shown the impossibility of educational reform, and even of sustainable educational innovation, by focusing exclusively on just internal (that occurring within the school) or external (that occurring in relation to family or community life) factors in education. In particular, recent research has underscored the importance of the family-and of mothers, in particular-in school enrollment, retention, satisfaction, and effective learning.

Educated parents, engaged themselves in learning and with high expectations of their children, make a critical difference in their children's motivation and achievement vis á vis learning. More and more programmes have started to acknowledge these facts, and to give special importance to parental and community participation, beyond the conventional "participatory" roles-attending meetings, assisting with homework, or providing financial support. In some cases, parents' learning needs are addressed, sometimes together with those of their children. In others, parents and community members actively participate in management bodies, and in teaching/mentoring roles.

Literacy and reading activities have provided a fertile ground for many such activities. Involving parents and communities is increasingly acknowledged as a competence that needs to be learned and thus incorporated into the professional training of teachers and of education managers. More and more programmes are seeing their mission, not only in terms of educating youth, but in actively engaging and enhancing learning among families and communities.

## Youth as Social and Change Agents

Youth are important agents of change in all societies, even if their contributions remain hidden from public awareness. Millions of youth worldwide study and work hard, take care of their siblings, assist those who know or have less, give up personal comfort to comfort others, and are actively engaged in cultural, social, and political action in their communities and countries. Adult literacy programmes worldwide, particularly in the South, have relied on youth as an important-and often as the main-teaching force. All over the world, one finds adolescents and youth as teacher aids and assistants in the classroom or in the school, in community libraries, health and community centers.

Today, youth are playing a critical role in helping children and adults, including their own parents and teachers, become familiar with modern information and communication technologies. Studies show that youth are enriched and gratified through work in service to their communities. Thus, it may be wise not only to invest in education programmes addressed to empower and enhance the self-esteem of youth, but to involve youth in activities in which they feel socially useful, dignified in their role, gratified by others' acceptance, and proud of themselves. As is well known by those who believe in the educative and healing power of volunteer and community service, young people who are given the opportunity to engage in the solution of real social problems, begin to engage in the solution to their own problems.

Teaching has traditionally been associated with adults and learning with children and youth. The traditional education relationship-at home and in all educational institutions-has been hierarchical and age-dominated. School systems were designed and have operated until recently with the assumption that what is learned in school is essentially prescribed in the curriculum and taught by teachers and textbooks. Peer interaction, both within and outside the home and the classroom, has largely been ignored as a critical source of learning for children and youth. Moreover, school culture has discouraged and even punished peer interaction, viewing it as disruptive, rather than as facilitating communication and promoting teamwork and collaborative learning.

Both parents and teachers have found it difficult to accept that they learn from their children and students, and that children and youth know and possess valid knowledge. School and social systems have been resistant to acknowledge the reciprocity between teaching and learning, and the inter-changeability of these roles across generations. This scenario has begun to change over the past few years as a result of economic, social, cultural, and technological changes, but also as a direct result of renewed understandings and practices in the education field. It is increasingly accepted that lifelong learning applies to all and that all ages are good to learn, that learning does not start with the first day of school, that children and youth must be heard and respected, and that they have much to teach and share with their peers, families, and communities.

Education has traditionally focused on teaching as opposed to learning. By contrast, "learner-centered approaches" place the learner at the center of education efforts with their learning becoming the most important indicator of effectiveness and success. For too long, learning was associated with rote learning. Retrieving and repeating information was confused with understanding and with knowing. Non-learning has traditionally been attributed to students, their families, and social conditions, and hastily explained as "learning problems," with little attention to teaching and system problems.

A focus on learning places the learners-their specific needs and wants, contexts and conditions-at the center of all efforts and decisions. Not only the curriculum and the pedagogy, but all aspects of educational delivery-teacher training, calendar and schedules, spatial arrangements, administration, evaluation criteria and procedures-must respond to learners' and learning needs, rather than to those of administrative and teaching staff. It means ensuring meaningful and effective learning, and enhancing -rather than inhibiting-the desire to learn and to continue learning.

It means accepting the inseparability between quantity and quality, content and method, process and results, teacher learning and student learning. It means believing in the learners' potential to learn and to succeed, and thus accepting non-learning as an indication of the need to modify the system and the teaching strategies rather than as an indication of learning and learner disabilities. Educational institutions are much more common than learning institutions. Not surprisingly, radical innovations often flourish in the most difficult conditions, where the inappropriateness of conventional education and teaching models become most apparent.

Education has focused on content, that is, on what learners must learn. Effective learners, educational institutions, and programmes have traditionally been measured in terms of the amount of data and information learners can store and retrieve. Educators are provided with desired learner profiles and outcomes, lists of knowledge, skills, values, and attitudes to be achieved-such as critical thinking, creativity, self-confidence, problem-solving, conflict resolution, tolerance, leadership, entrepreneurship, environmental awareness, teamwork, and other positive qualities. However, much less attention has been placed on how such competencies and values are attained, if they are teachable, and, if so, under what conditions and with what strategies.

Increased attention to learners and learning has meant greater attention to the hows of education-that is, to the selection and combination of strategies, methods, and means. It has also resulted in the increasing realisation that how something is taught and learned is a critical dimension of the learning experience. Creativity, flexibility, and diversification of strategies and methodologies characterise most youth education and training programmes.Two elements are particularly prevalent: (a) the revival of arts in all its forms (e.g., music, dance, crafts, painting, theatre, acting, film, video); and (b) the incorporation of modern information and communication technologies (ICTs), as both means and content for youth learning and development.

The incorporation of arts and of modern technologies into the educational arena form part of a broader trend toward recognising that culture, joy, and creativity are integral components of education and learning. Both the arts and ICTs have come to be perceived as motors for creativity and imagination, and as tools for strengthening identity, self-expression, and communication, particularly among youth. Merging education and culture, science and sports, and traditional and modern technologies is a challenge that more and more educational institutions and programmes are willing to assume, experimenting and learning along the way.

### *Critical Learning and Thinking*

Today's global trends demand that young people be engaged learners and critical thinkers. In the face of rapid changes, young people need to learn skills related to flexibility, teamwork, entrepreneurship, autonomy, creativity, and problem solving. Critical and autonomous thinking are more vital than ever for personal and social development. Access to information and modern technologies is not enough. Learning to identify, discriminate, and critically analyse information has become a key basic learning need in itself.

Social and economic realities are deteriorating for the majority of the population, and environmental degradation has become a serious threat to the future of mankind. Under these circumstances, active and responsible citizenship implies not only "adapting" to change, but also anticipating change, participating, controlling, and re-directing it through transformative social action.

But "educating future citizens" also adopts different meanings in youth education programmes worldwide, the main difference lying in the understanding of what it is to be a citizen and how youth are expected to play such a role. For some, citizenship and citizenship building mean learning about rules and obligations, democracy and participation; for others, it means engaging youth in voluntary or community activities; for others, it means developing critical and reflective abilities and capacities for self-determination and autonomy. Leading education institutions and programmes worldwide are engaged in this transformative understanding of education and learning.

***Promoting Students' Hehaviour***

Youth have traditionally been viewed as a problem by the adult society. Adults often think of youth as selfish, alienated, and prone to antisocial and negative hehaviours. The school system and mass media have become two major propagators of such negative perceptions of youth. The school contributes strongly with the image of failure: millions of children and youth enter the system as students and become slow learners, repeaters and dropouts. Some are given a second chance, with remedial and compensatory measures.

The mass media, while paying increased attention to youth and to youth issues, insist on stereotyping youth as frivolous and in highlighting youth delinquency much more than youth contributions to society. Studies in many parts of the world have shown the positive relationship between the high expectations of the parent and of the teacher, and young learners' self-esteem, performance, and achievement. Some studies conclude that high teacher expectations can have a more decisive impact on student learning and success than professional qualifications and experience. Other studies show that successful students coming from poor economic, social, and cultural environments have strong and determined mothers who believe in them and in their capacities, and who do not necessarily have a strong education background or even school experience.

Thus, for both teachers and parents, it seems to be the attitude, rather than the diploma per se, what makes the difference. Deficit approaches to learners lead to policies and programmes concerned with reeducating them rather than with educating them. More effort appears to be devoted to controlling or redirecting youth hehaviour, than in strengthening and developing good hehaviours, assets, and talents. As much as deficit theories and assumptions have been criticized and rejected in the education field, they remain alive, are visible in both rhetoric and practice, and continue to defeat the best intentions, particularly when dealing with the "disadvantaged"-those in developing countries, the poor, girls and women, and children and youth in difficult circumstances.

There's a big difference between "preventing school failure" and "ensuring school success." The first assumes failure as an outcome that can be avoided, while the latter assumes success as a possibility that can be reached. The first will strive for school retention and completion as indicators of success; the latter will strive for excellence. The first tells children, youth, and their families that they are prone to fail; the latter reminds them that they are meant to succeed. Working toward success implies different mindsets and efforts from all involved.

Fortunately, more and more programmes-and many of those portrayed here-adopt the "ensuring success" perspective.Translating this vision into coherent practice requires structural changes and a holistic strategy, and thus sustained efforts over time.

## Education for Work

"Education for work" has traditionally meant "education to get a job" in exchange for some monetary income.Technical and vocational education and training (TVET) have been based on the concept of employment. However, the situation and prospects of work have changed considerably. The future world of work will be increasingly knowledge-based and technologydriven. Technology is replacing labor, and thus it is expected that more individuals will shift to self-employment and to entrepreneurial activities. The employability of high school and even higher education graduates is no longer a given.

Unemployment rates have increased and continue to increase in most countries in the world, and a growing number of people cannot satisfy their basic needs through formal sector income alone. This opens critical challenges to school and training systems, and demands a radical re-thinking of TVET. The priority will be to ensure that children and youth develop competencies for sustainable livelihoods aimed at solving basic needs (e.g., living conditions, health promotion, personal services and care, social interaction, and entertainment). The experience developed by Enda Tiers Monde, a large international NGO based in Senegal, is highly inspiring in this regard.

**Formal and Non-formal Education**

Relevance has been at the center of educational debate both in the field of formal and non-formal education.What should children, young people, and adults learn? How and with what criteria should teaching and learning content be selected, when there is so much to be taught and to be learned? These questions are particularly critical when it comes to basic education, and to the education of the poor. Many place value on learning about oneself and one's immediate reality, and gaining knowledge and skills that have concrete and practical applications.

They doubt the relevance of literature and poetry, and even of history and world geography, for children and youth struggling for survival and confined in marginal neighborhoods or isolated rural areas. In fact, such minimalist approaches have commonly shaped education policies and programmes targeting the poor and other discriminated social groups. Emphasis has been placed instead on providing basic literacy and numeracy skills for all, domestic-related content (teaching girls how to sew), and farm-related skills for those living in rural areas.

Narrow approaches to basic education and to "basic learning needs" are under question today. More and more, equity has been placed at the center of educational debates and understood as making sure everyone gets similar learning opportunities, despite starting from tremendous disparities. Globalisation and modern technologies have broadened the world for all, not just for a minority. Lifelong learning is a need for all, and not just for a few. The present generation of children and youth, no matter who they are, where they live and what their future prospects may be, are already global citizens.

The concepts of relevance and of basic learning needs have been drastically redefined over the past few years. Policies and programmes that are leading the way have understood this, and have consequently expanded their horizons together with the expansion of information, communication, and learning opportunities. Study tours, visits, and internships (in the same country or in other countries), have been incorporated as regular components of student and teacher education and training programmes in many countries. Children, youth, parents, teachers, and entire communities have been involved in experimentation with ICTs, distance education, and e-learning.

Networking, on-line and face-to-face, has become a regular communication and learning tool for the education community, including children and youth, parents, teachers, schools, universities, NGOs, and local communities. While attempting to address specific segments or groups of the population, institutions and agents involved with the education and training of youth became increasingly specialised. One may categorise them by types of institutions school, out-of-school), ages (adolescents, youth, specific age groups, etc), gender (boys, girls), specific groups (e.g., street children, abused children, disabled, pregnant teens, out-of-school youth, drug abusers, prostitutes), topics and emphases (e.g., personal development, work skills, reproductive health, the environment). In general terms, four major goal areas can be identified in current programmes addressed to youth:

a) personal development,

b) social development,

c) school/academic achievement, and

d) the world of work.

Most programmes focus on one or two of these dimensions. However, holistic and comprehensive approaches to youth development are gaining ground. Fragmentation and specialisation have been counterbalanced with new groupings and alliances. A new term and a new professional category-Social Educators-emerged in recent years in an attempt to merge a wide range of educators dealing with specific groups and coming from three main areas: adult education, cultural promotion, and specialised education. New organisational arrangements have resulted from the emergence of new groups and issues, and the softening of traditional boundaries between disciplines.

The conventional classification of education into formal (that provided by the school system, organised in a given sequence, and with official recognition), non-formal (education activities organised out of the school system) and informal (casual or intentional, everyday learning that takes place without the mediation of education) has lost ground and is under question. Cross-sectoral interventions have become more common, especially those linking education with health, work, environmental, and gender issues. More common are collaborative efforts between governmental and non-governmental institutions, the public and private sectors, as well as between various governmental units and between international development agencies.

## Dropouts of School

Many programmes today are addressing the growing

problem of school dropouts. Retention rates in secondary schools are low and an issue of increasing concern. Poverty and other related factors-unemployment, family disintegration, child labor, or teen pregnancy-explain only part of this phenomenon. The other part is explained by the many problems school systems experience in attracting and retaining youth. As many have argued, the very term dropout may not be the most appropriate, given that often what is at stake is not so much an individual decision to leave but an institutional pressure that forces out.

Dissatisfaction, boredom, and lack of interest in what is taught and learned, are expressed by youth in relation to the school system all over the world.While this is true for young people in general, it is accentuated for students who do not respond to the standard student profile prefigured by school systems. Children and youth who have a home and a family and/or who do not have to work or take care of their siblings can dedicate special time to study and to play. Children who have educated parents, fathers who earn a regular income, and mothers who stay at home and assist with school work, also have a great advantage.

Many institutions and programmes dealing with out-of-school youth set "going back to school" as a key goal. However, going back to the same school will not necessarily ensure that things will go better this time, and youth know it. Grade repetition does not ensure learning and is, together with poverty, the most important predictor of school dropout.

The experience of failure, and of self-inflicted guilt for such failure, sets the stage for repeated failure, especially if the host institution remains unquestioned and unchanged. The "go back to school" appeal often responds to the common assumption that school failure is in reality, unilaterally, student failure. In cases where the school is found to bear some responsibility, there is a preference to not engage in what many see as an impossible battle:

reforming the school. Many, however, are ready to take up the challenge and work simultaneously on both fronts: with youth and with schools, with parents and teachers, helping build bridges and dialogue between them.

The concept of non-formal education (NFE) was born out of insufficiencies within and criticism of the formal educational system. The term non-formal education became associated with out-of-school education and was applied to a particular approach to education characterised by greater adaptation to the needs and circumstances of learners, creative use of educational resources, community participation, decentralised and more flexible organisation and management, and less authoritarian management and teaching styles.

Over time, formal and non-formal education, often opposed rather than complemented each other.Many saw out-ofschool education as the natural place for innovation and for diversification of education and learning strategies, and in-school education as inherently rigid, homogenous, static, and resistant to change. This situation, however, does not hold anymore. School systems have been experiencing innovation and important changes over the past few years.

In many countries- particularly in Asia and Africa- the term non-formal is also used today to refer to schools and school education policies and programmes that feature some of the characteristics once attributed to NFE and out-of-school education. NFE practice has also shown it is very difficult to transform conventional educational thinking and practice even outside school doors. Building bridges between NFE and FE, rather than developing them as separate systems, has been and continues to be an important goal in many parts of the world.

The distinction between formal and non-formal education has become unclear, and to a certain extent, irrelevant. In fact, formal (school education), non-formal (out-of-school education), and informal ("learning from life") learning converge in the lives of people. It is to be expected that in the next few years, and within the lifelong learning paradigm, conventional classifications will regroup around new categories. Education and training will be inseparable, knowledge and skills will fuse, and the "education" needs and opportunities will stretch along one's entire life.

Content will evolve constantly and so will the education and training demands of people. All over the world, education programmes exist that resist traditional classifications. They are challenging the formal/non-formal, school/out-of-school barriers, building bridges and creating hybrids in the effort to utilise all the opportunities and resources available to reach children and youth and make lifelong learning a reality for all.

***Documention and Evaluation***

Lack of documentation and lack of evaluation have been chronic deficits in the education field, and specifically in the field of educational innovation. Many good and even extraordinary experiences remain hidden, untold, and unanalysed, even for and by the people participating in them. The Action-Reflection-Action methodology needs to be a built in component of everyday work; yet this remains a challenge for educational innovators.

Documenting allows others to know and learn about the programme, but above all it allows programme participants to learn from it. Documenting is important for posterity, but it is essential for the present and for ongoing critical reflection on action. Evaluation is essential to knowing whether a given action is effective or not, to introduce improvements, and to build internal and external credibility. This same study has brought to the surface the weaknesses of documentation and evaluation efforts of youth education programmes. Very few of the over 150 programmes consulted have been thoroughly documented and evaluated.

Many more are documented than evaluated. And of those documented, very few go beyond the descriptive level and present a full account of the experience, sources of inspiration, its history and development, its achievements and obstacles, its assets and dilemmas, its results, and its ongoing and future challenges. Often, accounts are linear and anecdotal, and miss the most relevant or innovative aspects of the programme.

Also, most stories are told in writing, many of them have no pictures or visual resources, few have videos, and very few have a full combination of media, including books and other publications, videos, web pages, or CD Roms. Even "wealthy" programmes have poor documentation and evaluation results. At the same time, there are poor and under-financed programmes with very thoughtful and comprehensive accounts of what they did and do.

# 7

# Old-age Settlement Problems and Issues Related to Social Security

Social Security is both a concept as well as a system. It represents basically a system of protection of individuals who are in need of such protection by the State as an agent of the society. Such protection is relevant in contingencies such as retirement, resignation, retrenchment, death, disablement which are beyond the control of the individual members of the Society. Men are born differently, they think differently and act differently. State as an agent of the society has an important mandate to harmonise such differences through a protective cover to the poor, the weak, the deprived and the disadvantaged.

The concept of social security is now generally understood as meaning protection provided by the society to its members through a series of public measures against the economic and social distress that otherwise is caused by the stoppage or substantial reduction of earnings resulting from sickness, maternity, employment injury, occupational diseases, unemployment, invalidity, old age and death. The ILO concept of social security is based on the recognition of the fundamental social right guaranteed by law to all human beings who live from their own labour and who find themselves unable to work temporarily or permanently for reasons beyond their control.

At the international level, the preamble of the Constitution of ILO also referred to the need and protection of workers against sickness, disease and injury arising out of their employment, pension for old age, protection of the interests of the workers who were employed in countries other than their own. Thus, the right to Social Security was recognised officially for the first time. Subsequently, the UN General Assembly, while adopting the Universal Declaration of Human Rights also recognised the right to Social Security by stating that every member of the society has a right to social security.

"Social Security" has been recognised as an instrument for social transformation and progress and must be preserved, supported and developed as such. Furthermore, far from being an obstacle to economic progress as is often said, social security organised on a firm and sound basis will promote progress, since once men and women benefit from increased security and are free from anxiety, will become more productive.

There is considerable controversy about the social and economic effects of social security, and most of the current debate is focused on its supposedly negative effects. Social Security is said to discourage people from working and saving to reduce international competitiveness and employment creation, and to encourage people to withdraw from the labour market prematurely. On the other had, social security can also be seen to have a number of very positive economic effects. It can help to make people capable of earning an income and to increase their productive potential; it may help to maintain effective demand at the national level; and it may help create conditions in which a market economy can flourish, notably by encouraging workers to accept innovation and change.

A formal social security system presupposes the interventionist role of the State on redistribution grounds. Social security measures are generally income, maintenance measures intended to provide a minimum living to the people when they are deprived of the same due to invalidity, unemployment or old age. The two basic elements of social security are provision of a minimum living to those who are deprived of the same and 'selective redistribution of income' to a target group to reduce inequalities.

Social security to the workers would involve providing or framing such schemes or services or facilities and amenities, which can enable the workers to lead a decent minimum standard of life and having financial/ economic security to fall back upon in the event of loosing job for whatsoever may be the reason in the circumstances beyond their control. The workers must be given the wages and other services, which will enable them and the members of their family to lead a decent life. Thus Social security is an instrument for social transformation and good governance.

According to the ILO- World Labour Report-2000, the total security expenditure in India as percentage of GDP in 1996 was 1.8 whereas for the corresponding period the Social Security expenditure in Sri Lanka was 4.7, Malaysia 2.9 and China 3.6. In Argentina, the social security expenditure for the same period as a percentage of GDP reached the level of 12.4 and in case of Brazil 12.2. In comparison to Argentina and Brazil, the expenditure on social security in India is much less. The expenditure on social security cannot be directly related alone to the economic development. Intervention of the State would be essential and a co-relationship may have to be established for faster economic development.

Social Security in India was traditionally the responsibility of the family/community in general. With the gradual process of industrialisation/urbanisation, break up of the joint family set up and weakening of family bondage, the need for institutionalised and State-cum-society regulated social security arrangement to address the problem in a planned manner in wider social/economic interest at national level has been felt necessary. Currently, ongoing measures towards transformation process for trade and industry, increasing role of market forces and increase in longevity, in general world over has added a new dimension to the issue and enhanced the requirement further towards a planned and regulated institutionalised measure in the form of social security in its common understanding.

The social security legislations in India derive their strength and spirit from the Directive Principles of the State Policy as contained in the Constitution of India. Although the Constitution of India is yet to recognise Social Security as a fundamental right it does require that the State should strive to promote the welfare of the people by securing and protecting, as effectively as it may, a social order in which justice social, economic and political shall inform all the institutions of national life.

Specially, Article 41 of the Constitution requires that the State should within the limits of its economic capacity make effective provision for securing the right to work, to education and to public assistance in case of unemployment, old age, sickness and disablement. Article 42 requires that the State should make provision for securing just and humane conditions of work and for maternity relief. Article 47 requires that the State should raise the level of nutrition and the standard of living of its people and improvement of public health as among its primary duties. The obligations cast on the State in the above Articles constitute Social Security.

In India, out of an estimated work force of about 397 million, around 28 million workers are having the benefit of formal social security protection. Rest of the workers are in the unorganised sector. Several and successive attempts have been made in the past to address the multifarious problems faced by the workers in the unorganised sector through legislative as well as programme oriented measures. Even though these measures have not succeeded in achieving the desired object partly on account of the ignorance, illiteracy and lack of unionisation of workers on the one hand and the resource constraints of the State on the other, some of the programmes have provided a good setting through which the hopes and expectation of the workers in the unorganised sector have been considerably aroused.

A gigantic task of this nature would require a multi-dimensional, multilevel well integrated and efficiently delivered structural response would include legislation, its enforcement, enhancement of social awareness, involvement of voluntary organisations and committed individuals, while simultaneously improving the mobility, capability for better supervision and effectiveness of the enforcement machinery and of the schemes meant for the welfare of the unorganised labour. In the initial years of development planning, it was believed that with the process of development, more and more workers would join the organised sector and eventually get covered by formal social security arrangements.

The opening up of the economy, under the regime of economic reforms, has only exacerbated the problem. There is now almost a stagnation of employment in the organised sector with the resultant increase in the inflow of workers into the informal economy. The well designed social security system for the workers in the unorganised sector will help in improving productivity, contribute to the harmonious labour relations and thus to socio and economic development. It will encourage and propagate the social peace by reducing the frequency of industrial conflicts, increase the willingness to work, make it easier to meet delivery commitments and lead to improved quality product, a better investment climate and thereby enhancing the competitiveness of the economy.

The working group noted that the Second National Commission on Labour has been constituted by the Government to suggest rationalisation of existing laws relating to labour in the organised sector and suggest an umbrella legislation for ensuring a minimum level of protection to the workers in the un-organised sector. Effective enforcement of Social Security Acts through institutional mechanisms would impact on the level of trust and confidence of the working class. There is a felt need to look at the delivery mechanism in implementation of the Acts like EPF & MP Act, the ESI Act, Minimum Wages Act, Maternity Act, Workmen Compensation Act and the Payment of Gratuity Act.

The wage policy for the unorganised sector secured mainly through the Minimum Wages Act, 1948 is oriented towards providing a 'Need-based Minimum Wages'. In the unorganised sector, the wages are fixed under the Minimum Wages Act, 1948. The fundamental objective of minimum wage fixation is to improve the standard of living of those sections of the working population in the sweated sector whose wages are very low and whose living and working conditions leave much scope for improvement.

Under the Act both the State and the Central Governments are appropriate Governments for fixation/ revision of minimum rates of wages in the scheduled employments falling in their respective jurisdiction. The social security schemes in India cover only a very small segment of the organised work force, which may be defined as workers who are having a direct regular employer-employee relationship within a organisation. Out of an estimated work force of about 397 million, only 28 million are having the benefit of formal social security protection.

The Social Security Laws in India at present can be broadly divided into two categories, namely, the contributory and the non-contributory. The contributory laws are those which provide for financing of the social security programmes by contributions paid by workers and employers and in some cases supplemented by contributions/grants from the Government. The important contributory schemes include the Employees State Insurance Act, 1948 and the Provident Fund, Pension and Deposit Linked Insurance Schemes framed under the Employees' Provident Funds and Miscellaneous Provisions Act, 1948. The three major non-contributory laws are the Workmen's Compensation Act, 1923, the Maternity Benefit Act, 1961 and the Payment of Gratuity Act, 1972.

## Workmen's Compensation Act, 1923

The Workmen's Compensation Act is the oldest of the social security legislations intended for the welfare of workers. At present, the Act is applicable to workers employed in 50 hazardous employment/ occupations. When it was originally enacted there was a wage ceiling for coverage under the Act. However, it has been subsequently, removed and the provisions of this Act are now applicable to all the workers including casual workers employed in industries etc. mentioned in the Schedule. This Act takes care of two contingencies namely disablement due to employment injury and death due to employment injury.

A lumpsum compensation amount is paid to the disabled worker or the dependants as the case may be during both the contingencies. The maximum amount of compensation for disablement is Rs.5.48 lakhs and for death is Rs. 4.56 lakhs. In case of temporary disablement monthly payments are made @ 50% of wages upto 5 years. It is an employer's liability scheme, which mainly relies upon the good behaviour of employers. Where the employers are enlightened or where there are powerful trade unions, the rights of the workers are protected and the compensations are paid as per the Act.

In all other cases there is a tendency to pay a nominal compensation or even to deny it. In such cases the only remedy available to the workers or the dependants is to approach the State labour Department concerned and seek their intervention which goes upto arbitration which is a time consuming process. Even after arbitration there is no way by which the State authorities are in a position to enforce the payment of compensation. Very often, it is seen that small employers even with good intentions do not have adequate funds to discharge their liabilities.

The lump sum payment, which the worker or the dependant receives, does not provide real social security. In our social conditions there is a tendency to spend the money immediately even on non-essential items. As a result the lump sum amount paid is spent within a short time and the worker or the dependants are again in dire financial straits. Even in cases where they manage to retain the money, due to lack of knowledge about proper investment, they do not get adequate returns. With the cost of living going up year after year the standard of living deteriorates due to reduced availability of resources.

In the case of periodical pensions, there is a system of indexing, which takes care of the adverse effect of increase in cost of living to a large extent. Such a provision is not available in the Workmen's Compensation Act. The Workmen's Compensation Act is not applicable to those workers who are covered by the ESI Act.

**Maternity Benefit Act, 1961**

This Act is applicable to every establishment being a factory, plantation or mine and to every shop or establishment in which 10 or more persons are employed. The State Governments may, with the approval of the Central Government, declare that all or, any of the provisions of the Act shall apply also to any other establishments or class of establishment, industrial, commercial, agricultural or otherwise.

Under this Act female workers are entitled for paid holidays not exceeding 12 weeks in the case of maternity and during this period they are eligible to receive full wages. There is also provision for pre-natal confinement and post-natal care free of charge failing which employer is liable to pay medical bonus of Rs.250/-. In the case of miscarriage, maternity leave is available for a period not exceeding six weeks. There is also provision for sick leave for a period not exceeding one month in case of sickness arising out of maternity. This Act is also based on employer's liabilities.

Like Workmen's Compensation Act, the actual implementation of the benefit provisions of this Act also depends largely upon the good will of the employer. Here also the implementation is not satisfactory. Where employers are enlightened or where there are powerful trade unions, the rights of the workers are protected and the compensations are paid as per the law. In all other cases, it is very difficult for the female workers to take advantage of the provisions of this Act. Not infrequently the female workers are discharged even well before their due date of confinement and they are not paid anything till they are fit enough to resume their duties.

**Payment of Gratuity Act, 1972**

Extending to whole of India, the Act applies to factories, mines, oil fields, plantations, ports, railway companies, and to shops and establishment employing ten or more persons. The Act came into force on 16 September 1972. Other establishments included by notification are Motor Transport, Clubs, Chambers of Commerce & Industry, Inland Water Transport, Local Bodies and Solicitors Office. This Act provides for payment of lump sum gratuity to the employees. Under the Scheme Gratuity is payable @ 15 day' wages for every completed year of service subject to monetary ceiling of Rs.3.50 lakh. In case of seasonal establishments gratuity is payable @ 7 day's wages.

The gratuity is payable in the contingency of superannuation, retirement, resignation, death or disablement due to accident or disease subject to completion of 5 years continuous service. The condition is however, not applicable in case of death or disablement. Like Workmen's Compensation Act and Maternity Benefit Act the Payment of Gratuity Act is also an employers' liability scheme. In the absence of proper enforcement, many of the provisions of this Act also are observed only in their breach. The financial constraints of small employers also add to the problems in proper enforcement.

**Employees' State Insurance Scheme Act, 1948**

The Employees' State Insurance Act, 1948 applies to non-seasonal power using factories employing 10 or more persons and non-power using factories and certain other specified establishments employing 20 or more persons for wages. Workers in factories/establishments covered under the Scheme and drawing wages up to Rs.6, 500/- per month are covered under the Scheme. At present, the Scheme covers 2.30 lakh factories and establishments 86 million employees at 655 centres across 22 State and Union Territories in the country.

As of now, the total beneficiary population stands at about 34 million. The Scheme is financed from contribution from employers and employees. Employees contribute @ 1.75% of their wages, while the employers contribute @ 4.75% of the wages of insurable workers. Low paid employees drawing wages up to Rs.40/- per day are not required to contribute. The State governments contribute a minimum of 1/8th share of the expenditure on medical care in their respective States. The Scheme provides the following benefits:

- Sickness benefit including medical care.
- Disablement benefit

- Maternity benefit.
- Dependants benefit in case of death due to employment injury.

Of the above contingencies, the first three occur during the working life of an insured person and due to the contingency there is either stoppage or reduction in the income of the Insured person due to sickness, maternity or disablement. In case of total disablement, the workers are sometimes not able to continue in service at all. Depending upon the contributory conditions, the worker is entitled to cash compensation for 91 days in a year when he becomes sick @ 50% of his wage. In case of 34 chronic and long term diseases an enhanced benefit @ about 70% of wage is available to the worker for a maximum period of 730 days subject to fulfilment of certain contributory conditions. This benefit is known as Extended Sickness Benefit and is available to workers who have been under ESI coverage for a period of two years.

The Insured person and his family members are entitled to full medical care from the day the Insured person enters into insurable employment. In case of maternity, the insured woman is entitled to maternity benefit @ of full wage for 12 weeks which is extendable by further 30 days if she is unable to attend to her duties due to ailment arising out of maternity. In case of disablement caused due to injuries sustained in the course of and out of employment, the Insured worker is entitled to receive wages @ about 70% of normal wages from the ESIC for the entire period during which he/she is undergoing treatment and is unable to attend to his or her duties.

Unlike sickness benefit, there is no limitation for the period during which the benefit is payable. There are also no contributory conditions. In case the disablement results in permanent, partial or total disablement, the workers is provided periodical payments for life depending upon the extent of loss of earning capacity and his wage at the time of sustaining the injury. In case of death due to employment injury, dependants benefit is available in the form of periodical payments to eligible dependants @ about 70% of wage of the deceased employee. The comprehensive medical care provided by ESIC to the workers and their family members is provided through a network of 138 ESI hospitals, 43 annexes, 1443 dispensaries and 3000 clinics of private medical practitioners in different parts of the country.

The medical care comprises of OPD treatment, investigations, specialists services, indoor treatment and super-specialty care wherever required. In addition, drugs and dressings, appliances are also provided free of cost. There is no cap on expenditure incurred on medical care of an insured worker or members of his or her family. The treatment is provided through ESI dispensaries/hospitals and panel clinics of ESI Corporation. In cases, where facilities are not available in ESIC Institutions, medical care is provided through tie-up arrangements with other Institutions run by public or private sector. In the case of employees who have retired from insurable employment after having been covered under the ESI Scheme for not less than 5 years, a provision for voluntary coverage is available.

Accordingly, the worker and his/her spouse may avail the full scale ESI medical benefit on payment of Rs.120/- per annum as contribution payable in advance every year. Like-wise, an incapacitated worker and his/her spouse, who has ceased to be in employment, can avail ESI medical care on the same conditions till the normal date of his/her retirement. During the last five decades of its existence, the ESI Scheme has been extensively reviewed by a number of Committees such as ESIS Review Committee (1966), the Estimates Committee of Parliament (1969-70), the Committee on Perspective Planning (1972), the High Powered Committee on Amendments to the ESI Act (1978), the ESIS Review Committee (1982) and Committee on Perspective Planning (1993).

While many of the recommendations of these committees were fully or partially implemented, a large number of recommendations still remained to be implemented. The main recommendations, which were not fully implemented mainly pertain to extension of the scope of coverage, restructuring of medical care system, organisational framework and granting functional autonomy to the ESI Corporation. Most of the Committees recommended substantial improvements in the scale and standard of medical care, accountability of State governments to the ESI Corporation, effective liasoning between the State govt. and the Corporation, entrusting the administration of the Scheme to the Corporation and removing deficiencies in the panel system.

The Committees also recommended phased extension of the Scheme to smaller factories/establishments as also to other sectors not covered under the Scheme. The Committee also recommended making of provisions in the Act to frame modified schemes/truncated schemes having different contributions and benefit packages to suit the requirements of different sectors of workforce. It was also recommended that exemptions should be granted very rarely and the power to grant exemptions should be entrusted with the Central Govt. or the Corporation.

**Provident Fund Act**

The Employees' Provident Fund Act was passed in 1952 to provide for institution of provident fund for the employees of factories and other establishments. The Scheme came into force from 1st November 1952. The Scheme is presently applicable to 180 industries/class of establishments employing 20 or more persons. Coverage under the Scheme is restricted to employees drawing pay plus dearness allowance not exceeding Rs.6, 500/- per month. At present

3.40 lakh establishments having 2.6 crore employees are covered under the EPF Scheme.

The Scheme is basically meant for security of workers after their retirement. It provides for lump sum payment of provident fund, monthly pension and deposit linked insurance. The basic rate of provident fund contribution is 10% of basic wage/salary and the higher rate is 12%. The basic rate of 10% applicable to 5 main industries namely, beedi, brick, jute, coir and guargum for the rest it is 12%. Out of the employer share of contribution, a sum equal to 8.33% of wages is diverted to pension fund account while the balance of employers share of contribution and employees share of contribution in toto is credited to the provident fund account.

The accumulation in the provident fund account of a member becomes payable for final settlement under following situations:

- On retirement from service after attaining the age of 55 years.
- On retirement as a result of total and permanent disablement rendering the worker incapable of working.
- Immediately before migration from India for permanent settlement abroad for taking up employment abroad;
- Termination of service upon mass or individual retrenchment;
- Termination of service under a voluntary retirement scheme; and
- Termination of job and remaining unemployed for over two months or leaving the job from a covered establishment and joining an establishment not covered by P.F.

**Employees' Deposit Linked Insurance Scheme, 1976**

The Central Government notified the Employee Deposit

Linked Insurance Scheme, 1976 effective from 1st August 1976. The Scheme applies to the employees of all establishments covered under the EPF and MP Act, 1952, who have been enrolled to the membership of Employees Provident Fund Scheme, 1952, or any other Provident Fund Scheme which has been exempted under Section 17 of the Act or paragraph 27/27A of the Scheme there under.

The Scheme is financed with the contribution from the employer of the establishment @ 0.50% of the wages of the employees. Until 15.11.1995, the Central Government also used to contribute to the fund @0.25% of the wages. The employees are not required to make any contribution. The Scheme provides for payment of assurance benefit, upon death of the member while in service; linked to the average balance in the provident fund account of the deceased member.

**Family Pension**

A Scheme of providing family pension in the event of premature death of the employee was introduced from 1st March 1971 for the employees covered under the Act. The Scheme was financed by diverting out of contributions to the provident fund, the employees share of contribution @ 1.16% of their wage with an equal amount of employers share. The Central Govt. also contribute @ 1.16% of the wages of employee to the family pension fund.

The benefit is payable to the widow or other dependants of the deceased member. The grant of family pension is subject to 3 months membership of family pension fund. As this Scheme did not provide pension on retirement, superannuation or on death after service, the govt. framed a new pension scheme called the Employees Pension Scheme, 1995.

**Employees' Pension Scheme, 1995**

The Employees' Pension Scheme, 1995 was introduced w.e.f.

16.11.95, the pension scheme is compulsory for all members of the family pension scheme. It is also compulsory for persons who became members of provident fund from 16.11.95. Minimum 10 years membership of the fund is required for entitlement to pension. Normal superannuation pension is payable on attaining the age of 58 years and at a proportionately reduced rate on attaining the age of 50 years. The Scheme also provides for monthly pension in the contingency of death, total permanent disablement etc.

The amount of monthly pension depends upon pensionable salary and pensionable service. On completion of 33 years contributory service, 50% of pay is payable as pension. The minimum pension for the widow is Rs.450/- per month and maximum may go up to Rs.2, 500/- per month payable as normal members pension on completion of 33 years service. Family Pension up to Rs.1, 750/- per month is also payable to the widow of the member who has contributed to the pension fund just for one month. In addition to widow pension the family is also entitled to children pension @ 25% of widow pension payable up to two children till they attain the age of 25 years.

The employees have the option to accept the admissible pension or 10% reduced pension with return of capital equivalent to 100 times of original pension. The Scheme is financed by diverting employers share of PF contribution @ 8.33% of wage to the pension fund. Accumulation of the ceased family pension scheme constitutes the corpus of the new pension fund. The Central govt. also contributes to the pension fund @ 1.16% of the wage. In case of Employees' State Insurance Scheme also, there is a wage ceiling limit as well as a cap on the threshold of employment strength. The expansion of ESI Scheme is dependent upon the willingness of the Stage Government to expand medical facilities to new areas in their State under the Act, the State Governments have been given the statutory responsibility for delivery of medical care.

During the last 2-3 years, the membership of the Employees' State Insurance Scheme has almost been stagnant. Unlike the Provident Fund Scheme, where the beneficiaries continue after they cross the wage ceiling, in ESIC, the Insured Persons are excluded from the scheme, when they cross the wage ceiling. In the approach paper of the Planning Commission on the 9th Five Year Plan it was stated that labour policy during the Ninth Five Year Plan will rationalise, simplify and integrate the labour laws to bring them in tune with the needs of the changing socio-economic scheme.

At the same time, the existing legislative framework will be strengthened to protect the interests of the labour in the unorganised sector. It was, inter-alia, stated that social security will be provided to workers both in the organised and unorganised sectors. An integrated comprehensive scheme of social security will be evolved by having a single legislation covering all existing social security schemes. The Group noted that the recommendations of the Wadhawan Committee has been referred to the Second National Commission on Labour for an in-depth study. The recommendations of the Task Force would be considered for implementation as soon as the recommendations of the Labour Commission become available to the Government.

In such circumstances the Group felt that any major restructuring of ESIC and EPFO should await the recommendations of the Labour Commission. Under the ESI Act, the responsibility for providing medical care is vested in the respective State Government except in Delhi and NOIDA (UP) where the scheme is administered directly, by the ESI Corporation. However, the total expenditure incurred in administering the medical benefit in each State is shared by the respective State Government and the Corporation in the ratio of 1:7. The Corporation has issued norms and guidelines both for staffing and equipping ESI hospitals under the Scheme.

Under the above provisions it is the responsibility of the State Government to ensure availability of drugs, posting of specialists, medical officers and para-medical staff in the ESI Hospitals. Despite this, the health delivery system has not been found satisfactory. The State Governments have their own limitations in ensuring a reasonable medical care to the insured persons. The Corporation, with a view to improving the health delivery system has set up a Revolving Fund. It has been also proposed to set up a model ESI hospital in each State.

Under an action plan state government are being assisted in upgrading the facilities in the ESI hospitals. All these measure have not been able improve the health delivery system up to the desired level. There is need to further improve and simplify the health delivery system. Privatisation of health delivery system in selected hospitals may be required in the overall interest of the insured persons. Besides ensuing quality treatment, it would generate revenue for the Corporation which could be utilised for improving the services in hospitals and optimum utilisations of the existing infrastructure.

The Employees' Provident Fund Organisation has initiated a proposal for organisation wide IT reforms. It is proposed to issue 'smartcards' to the PF subscribers and allot a unique number which would improve the Provident Fund delivery system in the organisation. Considering the size of the subscribers in the PF, capacity building of the organisation would need special attention in the coming years. During the last 50 years, the Employees' Provident Fund Scheme and the Employees' State Insurance Scheme have been implemented to provide health, insurance, provident fund and pension for old age. These schemes were conceived immediately after independence, but did not fit into a clear policy frame work.

In view of globalisation and the economic reforms, it is now necessary to have a clear national policy on the provision of social security to different groups of workers and employees in the country. The policy could address the following issues:

- Whether social security is to be provided only to persons who are economically weak or should the social security cover be provided to other groups also? In most developed countries, social security is not confined to economically weaker groups alone.
- The extend of social security to be provided may be clearly defined i.e. whether the social security cover will be provided only for medical care and health, for the productivity of workers and for old age or whether this will also extend to persons who are unemployed and or are retrenched.
- The threshold for coverage under various schemes for social security and extent of coverage may have to be defined.
- Other social assistance programmes for specific groups such as handloom weavers, artisans, rural etc. should be dovetailed with the national social security schemes. At present there is duplication in schemes.
- The responsibility for implementation of various schemes for social security will also have to be spelt to avoid duplication of efforts at the Centre and State level. The institutional framework for effective implementation and the coordinating role to be played at the level of Centre and the State should also be spelt out.
- The strategy for implementation, whether a centralised or decentralised approach would be followed, should be formulated, for best use of resources.
- Suitable legislative framework for effective implementation for accountability at each level should be developed. The Centre could consider developing some model legislation in this regard.

- On the question of funding of security programmes, a consensus should be arrived at, keeping in view the long term sustainability of social security schemes. The question of what the Centre and the States can afford and what can be contributed by the beneficiaries and the private sector, should be worked out. Short populist schemes of social assistance may not offer and long term solution as social security addresses long term distress groups, during ill health, unemployment, old age. The possibility of levy of cess tax, incentives could be considered for funding.
- Standard packages for different target groups should be available throughout the country, since there is large scale movement of workforce and population from one state to another.

Pending finalisation of the policy on social security, during theTenth Five Year Plan, the strategy on social security could focus on; Pension, Accident benefit and Medical care in both the organised as well as the unorganised sector.

A sizeable number of workers engaged by various contractors for the purpose of loading/unloading, running canteen facilities, doing cleaning and sweeping of the premises, rendering security services etc. have remained out of the ambit of the ESI Scheme on the ground that they are working in premises which are not covered by ESI Scheme such as Railway stations, harbours, port trusts, Airports and various Central Public Sector Units engaged in non manufacturing activities etc. Steps should be taken to assess their number and to implement the various social security schemes in such areas so that these contract workers are able to derive social security benefits especially since many of such workers are unskilled and have no security of employment.

The coverage under Social Security is about 10% of the working population mostly in the organised sector. The vast majority of the workforce is in the unorganised sector, which includes agricultural labour, cultivators, small traders and hawkers, artisans and other self-employed persons, porters, auto-rickshaw drivers and other transport workers etc. Bringing them under formal social security coverage has been found difficult due to the following reasons:

a) Seasonal and intermittent nature of work, leading to difficulties in meeting the qualifying conditions.

b) Low level and irregular pattern of earnings and employment;

c) Absence of employer-employee relationship leading to difficulties in determining the principal employer and in assessing and recovering contributions.

d) Relatively weak administrative structure, particularly in rural areas.

Under the Employees State Insurance Scheme and Employees' Provident Fund Scheme a very small segment of workers in the unorganised sector are covered. The huge gap in coverage in the unorganised sector would call for a fresh strategy to extend coverage of both the schemes to the unorganised sector in the 10th Five Year Plan. This may require plan support and marketing of specific social security programmes to cater to the needs of the workers in different occupations.

Recently, the Govt. of India has formulated a separate social security scheme for agricultural labour. According to the Scheme, if 20 or more persons come together to form a sort of group and volunteer to pay contribution to a social security scheme, matching contributions will be paid by the Govt. of India and certain benefits like health care, pensions etc. will be provided from the corpus. On the same analogy social security benefits like health care, accident benefits, maternity benefit, pensionary benefit etc. can be made available to groups of workers in the unorganised sectors who are willing to organise themselves into small societies and contribute towards a mandatory social security scheme.

As there is no separate employer to contribute and the Govt. may not be able to fully subsidise the Scheme, it would be necessary to bring down the administrative cost to the barest minimum. It will be preferable if the administrative cost is borne by the Central Govt. by funding from the Plan or State Govt. and the Schemes are run under the supervision of State Governments actively involving these workers' societies in the day to day administration of the Scheme.

The State can shape the social security systems and influence their effectiveness by adopting suitable fiscal policy. As investment in social security impacts on human resource development, it would be desirable to make a paradigm shift in funding the social security schemes from non-plan to plan. The Central Government at present contributes @ 1.16 % of the wages of the worker to the Employees Pension Scheme, 95 and the expenditure is met from non-plan funds. During the year 2000-2001, expenditure has reached the level of the Rs. 600 crore. Since investment in social security leads to productivity and a contented work force, during the Tenth Five Year Plan, the State support to the pension scheme should be from the plan sector.

## Unorganised Workforce

The unorganised workforce is characterised by scattered and fragmented areas of employment, seasonality of employment, lack of job security, low legislative protection because of their scattered and dispersed nature, lack of awareness and high unemployment levels, perceived mismatch between the training requirements and the training facilities available, low literacy levels, outmoded social customs like child marriage, excessive spending on ceremonial festivities leading to indebtedness and bondage, etc., primitive production technologies and feudal production relations are further impediments not facilitating these workers to imbibe and assimilate higher technologies and better production relations.

The unorganised Labour can be categorised broadly into four categories as follows:-

- *Occupation*: Small and marginal farmers, landless agricultural labourers, share croppers, fishermen, those engaged in animal husbandry, in beedi rolling beedi labelling and beedi packing workers in building and construction, etc.
- *Nature of Employment*: Attached agricultural labourers, bonded labourers migrant workers, contract and casual labourers come under this category.
- *Specially distressed categories*: Toddy tappers, scavengers, carriers of head loads, drivers of animal driven vehicles, loaders and unloaders belong to this category.
- *Service categories*: Midwives, domestic workers, fishermen and women, barbers, vegetable and fruit vendors, newspaper vendors etc. come under this category.

***Necessity of Social Security***

The unorganised nature of the workforce, dispersed nature of operational processes and lack of institutional back up reduces their bargaining power and their ability to take full benefits from the Acts and legislations enacted for their benefits. Further, low skill levels of this workforce provides little scope for them to move vertically in the occupational ladder to improve their financial situation. The growth of informal, unprotected work with shrinking formal employment compels the workers to bear an increasing direct burden of financing social needs, with adverse effects on their quality of life. That burden may also undermine the capacity of enterprises to compete with global economy. The existing social security arrangements in the unorganised sector can be broadly classified into four groups as follows:

a) Centrally funded social assistance programmes;

b) Social insurance schemes;

c) Social assistance through welfare funds of Central and State Governments; and

d) Public initiatives.

*Centrally funded social assistance programmes*

The centrally funded social assisted programmes include schemes for both rural and urban areas under the National Social Assistance Programme (NSAP), which has three components viz., National Old Age Pension Scheme (NOAPS), National Family Benefit Scheme (NFBS) & National Maternity Benefit Scheme (NMBS). Under NOAPS, the destitute old age persons having little or no regular means of subsistence from his/her own source of income or through financial support from the family members or other sources is eligible to get old age pension @Rs.75 per month.

In case of natural or accidental death of a primary bread winner member of the household qualifying to be below poverty line and contributing substantially to the total household income between the age group of 18 to 65, a sum of Rs.10,000/- is paid to the family of the deceased under NFBS. Under the NMBS, cash assistance of Rs.500 is provided to the women of household below poverty line and 19 years of age and above, upto the first two live births. During 1999-2000, financial assistance of Rs.608.81 crore has been released under the National Social Assistance Programme to cover 65.41 lakh persons under different components of the programme.

In addition to NSAP, other important scheme implemented by the Govt. to ensure creation of adequate employment opportunities to provide social security to the people in the unorganised sector are :

*Employment Assurance Scheme (EAS)*: The Employment Assurance Scheme (EAS) launched on October, 1993 in some parts of the country was extended to all rural Panchayat Samities in 1997-98. It envisages to create additional wage employment opportunities at the time of acute shortage of wage employment through manual work undertaken for creation of infrastructure by the rural poor living below the poverty line. It is a centrally sponsored scheme run on cost sharing basis between the centre and states in the ratio of 75:25. Under Employment Assurance Scheme, a sum of Rs.3357.8 crore was made available to the state governments during 1998-99 and it generated 4279.36 lakh wage days during the same period.

*Swaran Jayanti Gram Swarojgar Yojana (SGSY)*: SGSY was launched on 1.4.99 by amalgamating erstwhile, IRDP, DWCRA, TRYSEM, SITRA, GKY and MWS primarily to improve the family income of the rural poor. It covers all aspects of self employment and beneficiaries assisted through credit-cum-subsidy programme. During the year 1999-2000, a total of Rs.959.86 crores was utilised by the States out of the allocations made by the Central Government (Rs.1105.0 crores) and State Governments (Rs.367.33 crores). A total of Rs.1056.46 crores was mobilised through credit under the scheme. The total number of swarozgaris assisted under the programme during the same period were 933868 of which 44.32% were SCs/STs, 44.62% women and 0.91% disabled.

*Jawahar Gram Smridhi Yojana (JGSY)*: JGSY was launched on 1.4.99 by restructuring the earlier JRY to ensure employment of rural infrastructure and generate wage employment for unemployed rural poor. During the year 1999-2000, out of the total financial assistance of Rs.2243.16 crores released by the Centre and the State Governments, 2683.08 lakh mandays were created with an expenditure of Rs.2035.27 crore. In addition to these programmes implemented through the Ministry of Rural Development &

the Ministry of Urban Employment & Poverty Alleviation, the Ministry of Textiles also implements certain social security schemes for workers in the Handloom & Power loom sector.

The office of Development Commissioner for Handlooms, Ministry of Textiles extends financial assistance under a central plan scheme, the workshedcum-housing scheme which is having subsidy, loan and beneficiaries contribution components. The unit cost of Rs.35,000 of rural house-cum-workshed consist of subsidy of Rs.18,000, loan from HUDCO/financial institutions Rs.14,000 and weavers' contribution Rs.3000 whereas unit cost of urban house-cum-workshed Rs.45,000 consist of subsidy Rs.20,000, loan from HUDCO Rs.20,000 and weavers contribution of Rs.5000.

During 1997-98 to 2000-01, financial assistance of Rs.53.05 crore was provided for construction of over 60,000 workshed-cum-housing units to the handloom weavers. As a welfare measure, a centrally sponsored Thrift Fund Scheme is in operation for the benefit of handloom weavers. The member contributes 8 paise per rupee of wage earned and the Central and the State governments contribute 4 paise each to the fund. The benefits include temporary advance, partial and final withdrawals. The scheme is implemented through the Weavers' Cooperative Societies/ Corporations etc. during 1997-98 to 2000-01, a sum of Rs.13.91 crore was provided to cover 6.9 lakh weavers under the Thrift Fund Scheme.

The Health Package Scheme intends to ameliorate some of the health problems related to the profession of handloom weaving providing assistance for reimbursement of cost of medicine and treatment of diseases like T.B., Asthma, cost of testing of eyes and spectacles, supply of drinking water, maternity benefits and infrastructure for primary health care is in operation. A sum of Rs.14.26 crores to cover 2.37 lakh weavers under Health Package Scheme has been provided during the last four years. Two insurance schemes are in operation for the handloom weavers. The first one is a New Insurance Scheme implemented through United India Insurance Company for the benefit of handloom weavers wherein an annual premium of Rs.120 is shared by the central government, state government and the handloom weavers @ Rs.60, Rs.40 and Rs.20 respectively.

The benefits include Rs.10,000 in case of loss dwelling due to natural calamities or fire, Rs. 1.00 lakh in case of accidental death, reimbursement of hospitalisation charges upto Rs. 2000/- and maternity benefits.. The second one is a Group Insurance Scheme wherein an annual premium of Rs.120 is shared equally by the central, state government and the beneficiary and the sum assured is Rs 10,000/- only. A sum of Rs.3.67 crore to cover 8.27 lakh handloom weavers has been provided to the state governments under both the insurance schemes during 1997-98 to 2000-01.

Similarly, the Office of Development Commissioner for Handicrafts also implements Workshed-cum-Housing, Health Package and Group Insurance Scheme for Artisans. It also has a plan scheme to provide pension of Rs.1000/- per month at present to Master Crafts Persons unable to work due to old age. There is an insurance scheme for powerloom weavers also to cover the workers in the age group of 18 to 60 years, and earning Rs.700 per month. The annual premium of Rs.120 is equally shared by the central and state government. The insurance cover is Rs.10,000/- in case of natural death, Rs.20,000/- on accidental death in addition to the accumulated amount in the member's running account payable with the interest @ 11% per annum.

*Social insurance schemes*

The Social Insurance Schemes available to the unorganised sector are operated through the LIC such as Social Security Group Insurance Scheme- All persons in the age group of 18 to 60 years belonging to the 24 approved occupation groups i.e. Beedi Workers, Brick-Kiln Workers, Carpenters, Cobblers, Fishermen, Hamals, Handicraft Artisans, Handloom Weavers, Handloom & Khadi Weavers, Lady Tailors, Leather & Tannery Workers, Papad Workers attached to SEWA, Physically Handicapped Self-employed persons, Primary Milk Producers, Rickshaw Pullers/Auto Drivers, Safai Karmacharis, Salt Growers, Tendu Leaf Collectors, Urban Poor, Forest Workers, Sericulture, Toddy Tappers, Powerloom Workers, Women in Remote Rural Hilly Areas.

The premium under the Social Security Group Insurance Scheme is Rs.10 per thousand sum assured, of which 50% is paid out of Social Security Fund and rest 50% is paid by the beneficiaries or the nodal agency. The benefits available include payment of Rs.25,000 in case of death or permanent total disability or loss of limbs and Rs.12,500 in case of loss of one eye or one limb in an accident. During 1998-99, 1.28 lakh new lives were covered and renewed 47.72 lakh lives covered earlier under the Social Security Group Insurance Scheme.

*Janshree Bima Yojana*: The most important and comprehensive scheme that has been launched recently, is the Janashree Bima Yojana providing insurance cover of Rs.20,000 in case of natural death; Rs.50,000 in case of death or total permanent disability due to an accident and Rs.25,000 in case of partial disability. The premium for these benefits is Rs.200/- per beneficiary of which 50% of the premium i.e., Rs.100 is contributed from the "Social Security Fund" and 50% contributed by the beneficiary/state government/nodal agency. Janashree Bima Yojana is available to persons in the age group of 18 to 60 years and living below or marginally above the poverty line.

The scheme is extended to a group of 25 members or more. During 2000-01, the scheme covered 2.16 lakh persons. It has been observed that coverage under the scheme is very slow. Lack of awareness, problems in constituting workers into groups to take advantage of the scheme, non-availability of incentives to the agencies at the grass root level to organise the workers etc. are some of the reasons of low coverage under the scheme.

*Krishi Shramik Samajik Suraksha Yojana-2001*: Ministry of Labour in consultation with Ministry of Finance launched a Krishi Shramik Samajik Suraksha Yojana - 2001 through the Life Insurance Corporation of India w.e.f. 1.7.2001. The scheme envisage to cover 20,000 agricultural labourers from each of the selected 50 blocks/districts, taking at least one from each state over a period of three years during the first phase. The agricultural labourers in the age group of 18 to 50 years are eligible to participate in the scheme. The beneficiary will contribute Rs.365/- per annum whereas the central government will provide Rs.730/- per annum per beneficiary from the 'Social Security Fund' for the year 2001-2002.

The benefits available under the Scheme includes life-cum-accident insurance, money-back and the superannuation benefits. In case of natural death or permanent partial disability before the age of 60, beneficiary will get Rs.20,000/- and Rs.25,000/- respectively and Rs.50,000 in case of accidental death and permanent total disability. The member will get pension ranging from Rs.100 to Rs.1900 per month depending upon the age of entry to the scheme on attaining the age of 60 years.

The financial implication to cover one million agricultural labourers over a span of three years in 50 districts is roughly Rs.76 crore per annum. The extension of the scheme to other districts to cover 10 million agricultural labourers out of 74.6 million total landless agricultural labourers in the country may involve financial implication of Rs.850 crore per annum. During the 10th Five Year Plan, possibility of extension of the scheme to other districts of the country would be explored in the light of experience of the first phase of the scheme and availability of funds.

## National Policy for Older Persons

The Government has been increasingly concerned with the issues of ageing, health and income security during old age as well as its close links to the mental and emotional well being. The Poverty Alleviation Programmes directed at the aged alone cannot provide a solution to the income and social security problems of the elderly. Faced with such large numbers, it is imperative that the problem will have to be addressed through thrift and self-help, where people prepare for old age by saving accumulating through their decades in the labour force. The role that the Government can play in this enterprise is to create the necessary institutional infrastructure to enable and encourage each citizen to undertake this task.

As a culmination of this growing concern the Ministry of Social Justice and Empowerment commissioned the National Project titled "OASIS" ( acronym for Old Age Social and Income Security) and nominated an 8 member Expert Committee headed by Dr. S.A.Dave, former Chairman of Unit Trust of India, to examine policy questions connected with old age income security in India. As per the Report, a person will open a single Individual Retirement Account (IRA) with the pension system at as early a point in his life as possible. The account will provide the individual with a unique IRA number that will stay with the individual through life.

The individual would save and accumulate assets into this account in his working life, subject to a minimum of Rs.100 per contribution and Rs.500 in total accretions per year. Individuals would be free to decide the frequency of accretions into their accounts; there will be no pressure to make a fixed monthly contribution. The account would stay with the individual across job changes, spells of unemployment, and can be accessed at any location in India. The individual would always have access to an account balance statement showing his assets. Also, the individual would be empowered in having control of how his pension assets should be managed.

Finally, upon retirement, the individual would be able to use his pension assets to buy annuities from annuity providers and obtain a monthly pension. At age 60, an individual would be able to derive benefits from his retirement account. The pension system would require that the first Rs.2,00,000 of accumulations be used for buying an annuity and thus obtaining a monthly inflation-indexed pension of roughly Rs.1500- which is well above the poverty line. Beyond that, an individual would be free to decide how his assets should be deployed. This minimum mandatory annutisation level (of Rs.2,00,000) should be periodically revised to keep pace with inflation.

Premature cessation of accumulation (e.g. owing to retirement before age 60) would be possible only if 100% of the assets are annuitised. Other benefits include integration of a micro credit facility into the pension system whereby individuals can have access to the Funds in the form of a loan against their pension savings. The bank branches can disburse these loans upto Rs.5,000 provided the individual pension account has a balance in excess of Rs.10,000.

The premature withdrawal would be permitted once an individual accumulate Rs.2 lakh in the Individual Retirement Account (IRA). Such withdrawals to a maximum of 30% of the accumulated balance above Rs.2 lakh shall be permitted for housing, medical, expenses for serious illness or other grounds specified by the Regulating Authority. However, the recommendations of the Report are still under examination.

A very fundamental handicap in the matter of registration and coverage of eligible categories of workers under social security schemes, whether being run by Central Government agencies or State Government agencies is the lack of a national enumeration for the workforce. Even amongst the workers who are covered by different schemes in operation under control of Central Government or State government, no nationally unique number is prevalent or available. Each agency that registers such workers and delivers benefit allots its own separate number, none of which are nationally unique.

Given the context of the level of mobility in the country's work force of close to 400 million workers, it is critical that a worker must have a nationally unique number which is potable i.e. the worker carries the number permanently across locations, across work and across employment, whether in the formal or in the informal sector. Such number must have the appropriate algorithm and technical structure which will be able to detect a duplicate or identify a worker who files for registration a second time as a worker though he already has a social security number.

None of the Organisations that delivers social security benefit have a numbering system or a design structure that is even remotely adequate to meet the requirements of registering the workforce with a nationally unique number. The registering of the workforce is a key concern and a key pre-requisite for any social security or social assistance programme where accounts have to be maintained, workers identified and benefits delivered to the appropriate person. The EPF, which has the largest coverage, is faced with the problem of the same worker having multiple numbers resulting from change in employment.

Workers withdraw accumulated benefits entirely at the time of change in employment which defeats the very purpose of social security in the form of old-age income protection. There is an even greater need to establish a nationally unique number for the informal sector where job changes and migration are far more frequent. The basic reason for lower participation and buy-in into the EPF programmes from the migrant labour, the casual labour, the construction labour and other service sector labour in the lack of a nationally unique number and a single constant account for such member which is not linked to location or employment.

Even the proposals proposed under the OASIS report presume the allotment of a nationally unique number to the worker before the commencement of even the first contribution from him. Given the above ground situation, the Working Group is of the opinion that, as part of the Tenth Plan a key focus area should be to establish a single national enumeration in the form of a social security number for the workforce. This number should be used by all agencies of the Central and State Governments in the matter of delivery of social security benefits to workers.

Apart from the direct benefits at the operational level in the matter of collection, accumulation and accounting of contributions and distribution of benefits, valuable strategic data will be generated indicating information relating to the mobility of the workforce, gender issues, seasonal movement in relation work, family status, income levels etc. in the work force which can be the basis for any future policy formulation at the strategic level.

**Welfare Funds**

The Central Government through the Ministry of Labour, also operates at present Five Welfare Funds for Beedi workers, Limestone & Dolomite Mine workers, Iron ore, Chrome ore & Manganese ore Mine workers, Mica Mine workers & Cine workers. Source of funding of these Funds is collection through cess on mica export, export of iron ore, internal consumption of iron ore, manganese ore and chrome ore as well as limestone and dolomite. The welfare fund for beedi workers is being financed by levy of cess @ Rs..2 per thousand manufactured beedis. Income under the Funds has reached the level of Rs.97.78 crore in 2000-01.

Out of total collection of cess in 200-2001, share of cess collection on beedi has been 58%. These Funds are utilised to provide various kinds of welfare amenities to the workers in the field of health care, housing, educational assistance for children, drinking water supply etc. The medical assistance provided under the welfare fund includes purchase of spectacles to mine and beedi workers, reservation of beds in T.B. hospitals, treatment and subsistence allowance in case of tuberculosis, reimbursement of expenditure upto Rs.1.0 lakh for heart disease and kidney transplant, maternity benefits @ Rs.500/ -for delivery to a female beedi worker for first two deliveries and assistance for family welfare.

Group Insurance Scheme for Beedi Workers There are 45 million beedi workers in the country. The beedi workers are covered under Group Insurance Scheme providing Rs.3,000/- in case of natural death, Rs.25,000/- due to accidental death or total permanent disability and Rs.12,500 in case of partial permanent disability. The premium of Rs.18 per worker per annum is equally shared by the Beedi Worker Welfare Fund (BWWF) and 'Social Security Fund' of the Central Government. Integrated Housing Scheme for beedi and mine workers An Integrated Housing Scheme for Beedi/Iron ore/Manganese ore/Chrome ore workers, Limestone and Dolomite mine workers is in operation wherein subsidy of Rs.20,000 per worker or 50% of the actual cost of construction whichever is less is provided.

Welfare Fund for Building and Other Construction Workers There is Building and Other Construction Workers Act, 1996 enacted by the Central Govt. Most of the state governments are in the process of constituting Welfare Funds, framing the rules etc. The Act has provision of levying a cess and to implement the Scheme through the welfare fund for the benefit and welfare of building and other construction workers. The implementation of this Act and Constitution of welfare fund in the long run will take care of social security needs of the workers engaged in construction activities in the unorganised sector. Further,

Govt. is also examining the possibility of having a National Policy on Home Based Workers, which may provide broad framework to safeguard the interests of this category of workers in the unorganised sector.

An important thrust area identified by the Ministry of Labour, Government of India, is the social security of workers in the fish processing industry. These workers constitute an extremely vulnerable and exploited category and are located in about 400 fish processing units in 9 coastal states of the country. The vast majority of these workers are migrant women in the age group of 16 to 35 years. A Task Force of the Ministry of Labour earlier investigated into their living and working conditions has recommended that steps may be taken for constituting a welfare fund for their benefit. This welfare fund would be used for providing various kinds of social security and welfare amenities to such workers. Similar welfare funds could be constituted for the workers for the Salt, Tendu, Taddytappers during the 10th Five Year Plan.

In addition to the Central Government, a number of State Governments have also set up welfare funds for various categories of workers. The Govt. of Kerala have set up about 35 Welfare funds for different categories of occupations and sectors. These welfare funds cater to the needs of agricultural workers, auto rickshaw workers, cashew workers, coir workers, construction workers, fishermen and women, khadi workers, handloom workers etc. The Govt. of Assam have set up a statutory fund under Assam Plantation Employees Welfare Fund Act, 1959 for the benefit of the plantation workers.

Similar funds have also been set up in Gujarat and Maharashtra under Bombay Labour Welfare Fund Act, 1953 and in Karnataka under Mysore (Karnataka) Labour Welfare Act, 1965 and in Punjab under the Labour Welfare Act, 1965. The State Governments of Andhra Pradesh and Uttar Pradesh have also set up Welfare Funds for various categories of workers. All these welfare funds however, cater to a very small segment of the total workforce. In view of the change in the perception of the social security i.e. an essential input to the productivity rather than burden on exchequer, some state governments are making concerted efforts to extend social security to the workers in the unorganised sector.

For instance, the Govt. of Karnataka is going to set up a Social Security Authority of Karnataka and create a Welfare Board to cater to the needs of the 66 identified occupational groups shortly. Further, occupational groups can be added to it as and when the need be. The Welfare Fund will be created by levying a cess from transport vehicles, employers contribution, workers and the state government when there is no employer. The Fund created therein will be utilised to implement schemes and programmes covering pension, health, housing, insurance in case of death and disability aspects for the benefit of workers.

Recently, the Government of West Bengal introduced State Assisted Scheme of Provident Fund for Unorganised Workers (SASPFUW). The scheme covers all wage employed and self employed workers between the age of 18 to 55 years in the unorganised sector having an average family income of not more than Rs.3500 per month. Each subscriber worker contribute a sum of Rs.20 per month and equal matching amount contributed by the state government. The interest on the balance at credit of subscriber is also paid by the state government annually at the rate declared by the State Government. Total contribution along with interest has to be refunded to the worker on attainment of the age of 55 years. The scheme will have provision for loans and withdrawals from the fund as prescribed by the State government.

The government of West Bengal had identified 50 industries in the unorganised sector and 16 self employed occupations, of which 13 unorganised industries and 7 self employed occupations are being covered in the first phase. These industries include tailoring shops, establishments having less than 20 workers, bakery, handloom, construction, earthen pottery, stone crushing, auto repairing, etc. The self employed occupations include cycle rickshaw, head load workers, railway/street hawkers, auto rickshaw operators, mason and cobblers.

The Department of Agriculture (Mandi Branch), Govt. of Punjab implements a scheme financed from the funds available with marketing Committees/Boards to provide financial assistance to the farmers and labourers in case of death or injury by operating the agricultural machinery/ implements and undertaking other operations both at the level of farm or mandi since 1984. The scope of the scheme includes

a) Death or disablement to any farmer or labourer (Farm and Mandi) working in the agricultural machinery implements or arising out of the use of the said machinery implements in the state of Punjab.

b) Death or disablement to any farmer or labourer arising out of digging of tubewell in the state of Punjab or electric current while operating tubewell in the farm.

c) Death or disablement to any farmer or labourer while using the insecticides or pesticides in the State of Punjab or due to snake biting while working in Mandi/Field or watering the field.

d) Death or disablement to labourer employed in Mandi arising out of use of agricultural machinery implements.

The financial assistance provided under the scheme includes payment of Rs.75,000/- in case of death, Rs.30,000/- in case of partial disability such as loss of one leg, eye, arm or serious injury, Rs.45,000/- in case a farmer or labour lost both eyes, arms, leg, etc. Rs.7,500/- to Rs.22,500/- in case of loss of fingers and Rs.30,000/- in case of loss of four fingers which is treated as loss of one arm. The Group was apprised of the free medical check up camps being organised by the Government of Punjab.

The Government of Tamil Nadu introduced Tamil Nadu Social Security and Welfare Scheme-2001. These schemes cover manual worker, Auto Rickshaws and Taxi Drivers, Washer-men, Hair-dressers, Tailoring workers, Handicraft workers and Palm tree workers. The State government is planning to formulate scheme for handlooms and handloom silk-weaving workers, footwear and leather goods manufacturing and tannery workers and artists. State government has set up the goal and social security and welfare fund for the respective workers.

Every worker registered under the scheme for two years initially has to pay a sum of Rs.100 and every employer 3% of the wages payable by him to the worker employed to the social security and welfare board. The fees for renewing the registration is Rs.10. The funds are to be utilised for paying premium towards insurance coverage having provision of compensation of Rs. One lakh in case of death or loss of both hands, feet, Rs.50,000 in case of loss of one hand or one foot and Rs.25,000 in case of permanent total disablement from injuries other than loss of limbs or death.

The financial assistance is extended to the tune of Rs.10,000 to the nominee of the deceased worker in case of natural death and Rs.2,000 to meet the funeral expenses. Assistance of Rs.1,000 for the education of the son or daughters of the workers passing 10th Standard examination, Rs.1500 for passing plus two examination and studying in regular bachelor degree course and Rs.2,000 in case of post graduate course or professional course for every academic year is provided through the fund. A sum of Rs.2,000 is extended to the applicant or his son or daughter for marriage. Further, assistance is also extended for delivery or the miscarriage or pregnancy or the termination of pregnancy by a registered female worker to the extent of Rs.2,000.

In addition to Governmental efforts, several public institutions and agencies are also providing various kinds of social security benefits to selected groups of workers. Two of the outstanding examples are those of Self-Employed Women's Association (SEWA) and the Mathadi Workers Boards in Maharashtra. The social security experiments of SEWA started in 1975 with a demand from members for a maternal protection scheme followed by health care and child care. This was followed by starting of an insurance programme in collaboration with insurance companies.

The insurance scheme started by the SEWA Bank was based on a realistic estimate of the capacity of the members to pay the premium. An Integrated Insurance Scheme introduced by SEWA for its members, offers several benefits for a consolidated premium of Rs.45/- per annum. While SEWA itself provides some of the benefits, it works as a nodal agency to get cover under various policies separately for specific benefits from different insurance companies. The risk covered includes health costs upto Rs.1000/-, maternity benefit of Rs.300/- and payment of varying amounts upto Rs.10,000/- in case of natural or accidental death including disablement of the member or her husband.

The insurance scheme has turned out to be both popular and financially viable. The total coverage of SEWA social security scheme is about 50,000 women. The experience of SEWA reveals that in order to become effective, the social security scheme for the unorganised sector should be locally managed and controlled. Further, only such schemes will become viable which are need based and integrated with the economic activities of the local people. If poor people are supported through capacity building and necessary linkages are provided with their own economic activities the chances of success of social security efforts increased significantly. Further, it has demonstrated that, it is not only necessary to search new social security programmes but new social security organisations to run them.

Over the period, emphasis would be on development of social protection systems which aim to relieve want and prevent destitution by restoring upto a reasonable level of income which is lost by reason of inability to work or to obtain remunerative work or by reason of the death of the bread winner. Financing social security arrangement in a populous country like India is not an easy task. Therefore, reorientation to the approach providing social security on self sustaining and self financing basis with least assistance from the Govt. in association with Self Help Groups, Non Govt. Organisations has to be encouraged.

As strengthening of the social security cover generate confidence amongst the workers and enhance productivity, the entire range of social security concerns has to be addressed in the context of national development and economy. The impact of globalisation and economic integration, casualisation of labor had affected the workers more in the unorganised sector. It is time to organise the workers in the unorganised sector and provide them minimum social security that cover food security, health and medical facilities and pension, housing, benefits apart from accident and death in accordance with the availability of resources and minimum involvement of government.

The long run strategy may be to bring all workers in the unorganised sector under social security cover and assure them a minimum level of social security benefits in a phased manner particularly the -

- Old age pension
- Life insurance
- Maternity Benefits
- Disability benefits (accident compensation) and
- Minimum health care and sickness benefits

The 10th Plan approach could adopt a two pronged strategy.

a) Extension of existing Acts/schemes and programmes to cater to the social security needs of the workers.

b) Introduction of new programmes on self finance and self sustaining basis by involving the local bodies and workers themselves.

Main focus during the 10th Plan would be on : The Cooperatives, Self Help Groups, Mutual Benefit Association set up, managed and financed by the occupational groups/ workers themselves in the unorganised sectors would be encouraged to have voluntary health insurance and pension schemes. Identify the gaps, omissions, deficiencies in the existing social security arrangement and rectify the same.

Encouragement to bottom up participatory approach. Identification of mechanism where employers have to contribute towards the social security programme of the workers. Alternative income generating activities with provision of credit arrangement for supply of raw materials etc.

Convergence of schemes implemented by the various deptt. of the central/state government Organisation of awareness generation campaigns and dissemination of information to workers for the benefit of workers in the unorganised sector Improve efficiency of delivery mechanism of existing programmes to reach the workers in the unorganised sector. Emphasis to address educational, health and housing needs of the workers in the unorganised sector. Involvement of local institutions like civic bodies/ municipalities and Panchayati Raj Institutions for the implementation and monitoring of social security programmes.

Considering the size of the massive workforce in the country a policy frame work at the National level is needed on the provision of social security in the unorganised sector.

For the 10th Five Year Plan the strategy should be realistic and would focus on some minimum level of protection that could be translated into practice within the existing constraints. Therefore, the Social security could focus on Pension, Accident benefit and Medical care.

The State should come forward with more plan assistance on this important matter of social concern as a welfare state it cannot delink itself from this important obligation. It is crucial to build up social awareness as a compulsory measure to prevent exploitation of workers in the unorganised sector. Steps need to be initiated for inviting active participation from the voluntary organisations, trade unions and other committed individuals to build up such social awareness with the object of empowering workers who are currently vulnerable to exploitation of landlords, moneylenders and malfunctional and dysfunctional middlemen.

# 8

# Transformation of India into an Advanced Nation

The distinctiveness of the Indian experience lies in its history as a developing country. It also lies in the paradox that the university system, on which the country now depends for its advance as an independent nation, was initially designed to function as an instrument of colonial rule. The European system of higher education was introduced into India by the British, in 1857, with the establishment of universities for European education in Bombay, Calcutta, and Madras. Although modeled after the University of London, these universities were not meant to be institutions for the advancement of knowledge, or full-fledged centers of higher learning.

The British government had established them with two limited objectives: first, to introduce the Indian elite to European culture, and thus, to colonise the country culturally; second, to produce a cadre of Indians equipped to serve the British administration in India and to practice the professions of law, medicine, and teaching, as required by the British. All the three universities, as well as 18 others that had been established by the time India acquired independence from British colonial rule in 1947, were designed to serve these limited objectives alone. They were, therefore, different from their European counterparts. For instance, only disciplines such as history, philosophy, literature, the languages, law, medicine, and education, considered relevant to the two objectives, were taught. The social sciences, as well as technical and technological subjects, were neglected.

Facilities for studying science were restricted to the level required to produce school teachers and undergraduate-level college teachers. Facilities for graduate education and research-even in fields such as medicine and law-although considered essential, were practically unavailable. Those who aspired to graduate qualifications or specialisation were expected to go to Britain for further education. The emphasis on imbibing European culture and knowledge was so pronounced that universities never really encouraged a spirit of critical inquiry or independent thinking so vital to the advancement of knowl-edge.

India has an old tradition of knowledge and learning; in fact, a well-established system of higher education functioned as early as 1000 B.C. In this system, the construction of knowledge, the beliefs on which knowledge is based, basic concepts, and the organisation of learning are very different from the European tradition. But the system is validated by the fact that it sustained Indian civilisation for centuries. Initially, the British had accepted the indigenous system of knowledge, and allowed institutions for indigenous education to exist. But with the establishment of the first three universities, the British declared their preference for European knowledge, instituted policies that favored European education, and withdrew their support for indigenous institutions.

English was established as the only medium of instruction permitted for university education. British economic policy, similarly, withdrew support for indigenous crafts, skills, and professional practice, although India was highly advanced in fields such as textiles, architecture, waterworks, and medicine. Together, these two policies steadily created a climate in which indigenous knowledge was rejected and links with traditional learning were broken. Access to higher education was restricted because facilities were meager. In addition, British policies were self-consciously elitist. Whenever it was asked to expand facilities, the British government would argue that the benefits of privileges provided to the elite would eventually trickle down to the masses.

Elitism was also encouraged by the fact that instruction was only available in the language of the rulers. Universities were statutory bodies closely controlled by the government. Their structure and functioning were governed by a university act passed by the government. The governor of a province was the chancellor of all universities within the province under his jurisdiction. He appointed the vice chancellors, who were second in command and directly in charge of individual universities. Government nominees sat on the all-important bodies-such as the Senate, the Executive Council, the Academic Council, and committees for the selection of faculty and administrative staff.

## Indian Response

Indians valued European higher education as the means to acquire employment in the British establishment; to enter the professions of law, medicine, and teaching as practiced under British rule; and to gain access to European social circles. They valued the English language as a window on the Western world. And they acknowledged the fact that European education had inspired the nationalist movement for freedom. But they felt that policies pertaining to university education in India denied Indians the opportunity to advance, distanced them from their own culture, restricted economic growth, and bred continued dependency on Britain for knowledge.

The determination to free university education in the country from all these handicaps shaped nationalist dreams and aspirations for higher education in independent India. When India acquired independence, education was chosen to be the principal instrument for the country's transformation from a poor, dependent, economically and technologically backward imperial colony into an advanced nation. In the larger design for this transformation, which calls for economic development as well as extensive social and political change, higher education was charged with two major responsibilities.

First, higher education was to provide the manpower required for economic growth and for an efficient delivery of services such as healthcare, transport, communication, and community welfare-considered basic to a developed society-and to contribute to the advancement of knowledge in the manner required to place India on par with the developed world. Second, higher education was to function as an instrument of equality. It was recognised that these objectives were the very opposite of those that universities in British India had served. Nevertheless, it was believed by instituting appropriate policies and facilities it would not be difficult to gear universities to the new objectives.

## Knowledge Advancement and of Manpower Production

In order to enable them to advance knowledge and to produce the manpower required, universities in independent India have been equipped with facilities for undergraduate as well as graduate education, in the full range of disciplines available at universities in developed countries. At least one agricultural university has been established in each state. In addition, a new category of national-level apex institutions-such as the Indian Institutes of Technology (IITs) and the Indian Institutes of Management (IIMs)-have been established to provide world-class education in fields such as engineering, technology, management, and medicine, which are considered critical to development.

Several national-level institutions have also been established for research in different fields. All these new institutions have been established in consultation and with assistance from some of the best-known experts and institutions of higher learning in Europe and North America. The government has, thus, invested heavily in revamping higher education. India no longer depends on developed countries for higher education or for qualified manpower. It has the world's third-largest pool of scientifically and technically trained personnel. The products of Indian higher education are accepted for employment worldwide. Students from other countries, particularly the African countries, come to India for higher studies.

Until about two decades ago there was euphoria over all this. However, since then, serious problems have surfaced. For instance, highly qualified Indians, particularly the products of prestigious institutions such as the IITs, have been migrating to Europe, North America, and recently to Australia. Although referred to as the "brain drain," this phenomenon was initially celebrated as India's successful entry into the international market for employment. But it is now resented that, while the migrants prosper, the country is deprived of returns from its massive investment in technical, technological, and professional education. Institutions of higher education, particularly the apex institutions, are blamed for their failure to cultivate, among their students, a commitment to serve the country.

Even more serious is the problem of the underemployment and unemployment of graduates. This phenomenon is generally explained away with the statement that the economy has not grown at the pace, and on the scale, required to absorb all the manpower that the institutions of higher education produce. Yet, many positions in industry, in government administration, and surprisingly even in educational institutions, lie vacant for want of suitably trained persons. This is in part because qualifications for employment are narrowly and rigidly defined. But it is also due to a measure of mismatch between what higher education produces and what the country needs.

## Role of the Traditional Sector

The most disturbing aspect of this mismatch is that the products of the country's system of higher education are not adequately equipped to serve the traditional sector. This sector consists of occupations such as agriculture, farming, fishing, forestry, indigenous crafts, services, and trades, and accounts for 70 percent of the economy. Fifty years ago, when India chose massive industrialisation as the strategy for economic advance, it was believed that this sector would simultaneously modernise. But this has not happened. Occupations in this sector depend almost entirely on indigenous knowledge, skills, and technologies and traditional modes of marketing and management. It is now pointed out that the economic advance of the country hinges precariously on the development of this sector and that its knowledge, technology, skill, and manpower needs, hitherto neglected, must be urgently addressed.

The experience of some nongovernmental organisations (NGOs), that have made considerable headway in this direction indicates that addressing these problems is not easy. It shows that technologies transferred from developed countries need considerable adaptation before they work satisfactorily in this sector. Moreover, the people in this sector are unwilling to give up traditional methods and practices, particularly because many of these are deeply entrenched in sacred beliefs and customs. By interacting patiently and establishing rapport with the people, these NGOs have been able to enrich traditional skills with modern technologies and bring about substantial change. It is significant that they in turn have come to understand and appreciate the wealth of wisdom, experience, and knowledge underlying traditional practices and ways.

But firmly anchored in Western technology and thought, unused to interactive learning and teaching, and bound by structural requirements that are highly inflexible, university teachers and researchers in India have been finding it difficult to relate to this sector. Much the same happens with respect to the task of advancing knowledge in music, dance, philosophy, psychology, yoga, Ayurvedic and Unani medicine, architecture, astronomy, and a number of other fields where rich stores of knowledge and traditions of learning, banished by the British, now lie waiting to be revived and developed. Distanced from indigenous knowledge for more than a century, universities have been finding it difficult to relate to it.

### Global Advances and Market Forces

While higher education is thus challenged from the grassroots and by the indigenous culture, it is also relentlessly pressed to keep pace with global advances, in the development of both manpower and research. Faced with the competing demands on its resources, the government is unable to provide adequate funds to maintain facilities at the level required-even at institutions such as the IITs and IIMs, internationally recognised for the quality of education. There are other problems. For instance, in order to make their mark in their disciplines, Indian academics prefer to do research and to publish on issues that are of international import. These issues are not always relevant to the country's needs.

In the international network, they are often exploited by being invited only to provide data from the Indian subcontinent. Meanwhile market-driven demands force institutions of higher education to concentrate on the short-term objective of providing employment-oriented courses, at the cost of their mission to advance knowledge. Because there are few careers in research, very few good students opt for courses that lead to the advancement of knowledge. While the academic purpose is thus relegated to the background, there is no room for a good all-round liberal education either. More recently, with the liberalisation of the country's economy, global market forces have generated new fears and dilemmas for higher education in India.

In order to take advantage of the low cost of educated labor, multinationals have been locating many of their labor-intensive operations here. While institutions of higher education are pushed to produce appropriate manpower, observers are unsure about whether this will contribute to the country's economic progress or toward its colonisation by the economies of the developed world.

### Role of Higher Education as an Equality Instrument

To equalise access, the bottom line of the government's policy is to provide opportunities for higher education to all those who aspire to it. To serve this commitment, facilities have been massively expanded. Fees have been kept low. The vernacular languages have been introduced as the media of instruction. Several universities offer fee waivers to women students. Further, in a bold move to extend access to sectors of the population known to have poor access to university education, the government has instituted a policy of "reservations."

According to this policy, it is mandatory for all institutions of higher education that receive government funding (and almost all do) to reserve a quota of admissions as well as faculty and administrative positions (a) for the castes that are considered to be low in the caste hierarchy and that were therefore traditionally denied the right to education, and (b) for the aborigines or tribes who were traditionally excluded from education because they functioned outside the mainstream of urban and rural life.

Scholarships and other facilities have also been liberally provided for these two categories. Together, all these provisions have yielded spectacular growth.

In 1950-51 when the country's First Five Year Plan was launched, there were 27 universities serving 174,000 students. By 1997 there were 229 universities, more than 8,000 colleges, 6.4 million students, making India's system of higher education the second-largest in the world. To finance this expansion, the Government of India has consistently increased its share in the total expenditure on higher education-from 49.1 percent in 1950-51 to more than 90 percent today, although government allocations to education have declined to 3.8 percent of GDP, the lowest in South Asia.

It is significant that despite these impressive statistics the enrollment in higher education in India today accounts for barely 6 percent of the relevant age group, as compared to 30 percent in Europe and 50 percent in North America. This is partly because the expansion has been offset by the growth of the population in the relevant age group. Nevertheless, the fact illustrates how difficult it is for developing countries to bridge gaps and to keep pace with the developed world.

Although they have been increased phenomenally, facilities fall short of demand. For some professional programmes, there are more than 500 applicants per seat. The unrest this generates is so intense that in some states the government has had to administer admissions. To meet the demand, facilities are constantly stretched beyond capacity. As a result, quality suffers. For instance, when classes were small, teachers were able to encourage questions and stimulate interaction, in spite of teaching by the lecture method, extensively used in the country. But now, as they lecture to large numbers, this is no longer possible. Quality is also affected by the fact that few students are academically motivated. Most pursue a degree for the status it carries and because it is a required qualification for employment.

Students in the professional stream take courses that are relevant to their future work, and regardless of their initial attitude, many grow to be interested as they move on. But more than 70 percent of the students are enrolled in the traditional faculties of arts, science, and commerce, in courses that have little relevance to the occupations they will eventually take up. They are aware of this and therefore indifferent, certificate oriented, and examination driven, as are their teachers. Meanwhile, institutions are weighed down by the bureaucratic requirements of the government and their own rules and regulations, designed to cope with large numbers. As the academic purpose has thus receded in importance, malpractice and corruption have grown. Professional education, hitherto relatively safe from these forces is being slowly sucked in.

While quality and relevance thus suffers, equality does not fare any better. In fact, new inequalities have emerged. Professional education has steadily grown in prestige. Among professional institutions, the new apex institutions such as the IITs and IIMs are considered to be in a class apart. It is significant that the students who succeed in the competition for admission to professional courses in general, and to these institutions in particular, largely come from more well-to-do, educated homes and superior schools. The privileges of wealth are visible in the fact that both private colleges that charge hefty fees and European, North American, and Australian universities that peddle expensive courses have no dearth of students.

Another sign is the fact that parents who can afford to do so send their children abroad for further education. Until recently, this happened after completion of the first degree. Now, as quality declines and admission to better institutions has become highly competitive, many students are sent abroad for the first degree. The effort to provide equal opportunities for higher education is also defeated by the fact that facilities for schooling are highly uneven and unequal. Most significant is the fact that barely 65 percent of children in the relevant age group complete primary school and that less than 30 percent complete high school.

Reservations have enabled the disadvantaged castes and tribes to advance significantly, in education as well as in employment, but they have become highly politicised. For instance, the performance level of candidates admitted to reserved seats at institutions such as the IITs is significantly lower than the cutoff point for open admissions, but at-tempts to bridge this gap with remedial courses are rejected as discriminatory. In Parliament these institutions have been accused of trying to maintain international standards at the cost of addressing national realities. And most institutions of higher education are neck deep in litigation over reserved admissions, as well as reservation of faculty and administrative positions.

In the face of this scenario, higher education in India can hardly claim to have functioned successfully as an instrument of equality. Yet there is visible, as well as statistical, evidence of a complete transformation of the structure of opportunities in the country-for the traditionally disadvantaged castes and tribes, for women, and for the classes that not very long ago had little or no access to higher education, and to the futures that education opens up.

**Privatisation and Government Policy**

The expansion of higher education has been criticised and questioned, given the associated academic and social costs. But the government is unwilling to retreat from its initial promise, regarded by it as the realisation of the nationalist dream and as part of its basic obligation as the instrument of a welfare state. In a more pragmatic vein, the government recognises that people's aspirations for higher education are so intense that it would be suicidal to curb access. It is also driven by the ambition to achieve enrollments comparable to those in Europe and North America. This ambition is legitimised by the fact that bodies such as the World Bank consistently emphasise the high rates of return from higher education.

Finally, there is also the consideration that by expanding opportunities to improve qualifications it is able to contain the frustrations in society because of underemployment and unemployment. However, faced with public demand and political pressures to accomplish universalisation of primary school education at least by the end of the century, the government has finally realised that it cannot afford to subsidise higher education as it has for the last 50 years. At the same time, a section of the population clearly has the capacity to pay for the expensive higher education facilities provided by some private institutions and by foreign universities. The government is, therefore, considering privatisation.

However, it has two apprehensions. First, equality might be placed in jeopardy if the facilities available to those who are able to pay are superior to the facilities available to those who cannot pay. Second, higher education could be commercialised to the point that it is almost entirely market driven. The government is, therefore, thinking of extending a system already in operation in some states during the last decade. A large number of institutions of higher education in the country are owned and managed by private bodies. Most are "aided" with government funds that fully cover the costs of their maintenance and operation.

Regardless of whether they are aided or unaided, all private institutions charge the same fees. Moreover, in academic as well as administrative matters, all of them are very closely controlled by government and university rules and regulations. According to the system in place in some states, referred to earlier, selected and preferably new private unaided institutions are allowed to charge substantially higher fees. However, the amount has to be approved by the government. The selected institutions are given a few concessions in administrative matters. But, by and large, they are closely governed in the same manner as are other institutions. It is unfortunate that India is considering this brand of privatisation-one that does not allow for the space, flexibility, and freedom required for the advancement of knowledge, quality, and relevance.

There is much to learn from the Indian experience, particularly for developing countries, for countries served by European education but rooted in non-European cultures, and for countries making the transition from a fully state-supported education system to one being serviced by the market. European higher education implanted in non-European societies has often smothered or displaced indigenous knowledge, technologies, skills, values, and other elements of the indigenous culture. Developing societies with non-European cultures are now beginning to discover that it is not wise to anchor plans for development in European knowledge and technology alone. It is now recognised that indigenous knowledge, once dismissed as primitive, has much that is of global value, and deserves to be retrieved.

The market is a powerful force in making higher education relevant to employment. But like a cancerous growth, it can destroy love for learning, crowd out philosophical and literary pursuits, stifle the advancement of knowledge, and render both theoretical and liberal education irrelevant. With the globalisation of the economy, the developed societies tend to impose their manpower needs on the higher education systems of less-developed societies and to push the latter into the background. These problems have to be consciously addressed.

The internationalisation of higher education, generally understood as the intercountry exchange of students and faculty, has many other facets: the growth of an international market for educated manpower and the challenge to equip students with transnational competencies so that they can compete in this market; international partnerships and networking for the advancement of knowledge; the phenomenon of individual scholars as well as individual countries promoting their vested interests to the disadvantage of the larger endeavor; and the marketing of courses by universities in countries other than their own and consequent issues of ownership, partnership, accreditation, acceptability, and accountability.

The Indian experience clearly indicates that the traditional organisation of higher education into disciplines-particularly in the faculties of the arts, commerce, and science-has become largely irrelevant to the knowledge and skills needs of society. It reveals that higher education needs to be in close touch with the world of work and to interact with it meaningfully. It also illustrates that much that is vital to the advancement of knowledge and technology is happening outside the system of higher education. Higher education systems must find a way of linking to these developments. In several other ways, the Indian experience underlines the need to restructure higher education and to do this as part of restructuring the larger framework of secondary education, and with full awareness of societal realities and needs.

The Indian hesitation in the matter of the privatisation of higher education indicates that the challenge for the country is to function as a civil society and to substitute civil control for regulation by the state. The current situation with respect to the privatisation of higher education in India illustrates the anxieties of the transition.

# 9

# Innovative Professional Development Programmes

In India, first enterprising attempt was made by Maharaja Sayaji Rao Gaekwad, the ruler of Baroda state, who invited W.A. Borden, a disciple of Dewey, to improve library system of his state. For creating a cadre for the newly established public library system of Baroda state, Mr. Borden initiated training in librarianship in India in 1912. Therefore, Sayaji Rao Gaekwad and Mr. Borden are the two pioneers in initiating and teaching library science education in India. A D Dickinson, another student of Dewey, was appointed as the Librarian of Punjab University. Gradually other university and library associations started setting up library schools. The first certificate course in library science was started in 1929 by the Madras Library Association under the tutelage of Dr. S.R. Ranganathan, who is regarded as the 'father of library movement' in India.

At present, more than 100 universities and their affiliated colleges/institutions are conducting courses in library (and - now also- information) science at bachelors as well as masters degree. M. Phil and Ph. D is also offered by over 39 universities. In addition, a number of state level professional associations in association with their respective state governments also run certificate courses. A few university level institutions in India (DRTC in Bangalore,

INSDOC in New Delhi, NCSI at IISc in Bangalore) also impart specialised courses on areas like documentation, information science, library automation, information technology, management of information systems (MIS) etc.

## Continuing Professional Development Programmes (CPDPs) in India

In view of the challenges posed by the 'knowledge-driven economy', LIS professionals have not only to deal with greater quantities of information than earlier, but, using ICT, have also to change their role from passive providers of information support to more proactive providers of information itself. In keeping with this changing and ever evolving requirement, CPDPs for them are being organised by various agencies on several frontier areas that include the following:

- State-of-the-art exposure in ICT including, in particular, areas such as computers, communication, networking and Internet, multimedia, reprographics and micrographics, printing and publishing technologies, digital and electronic libraries,
- consortia initiatives, and the web world.
- Exposure to latest sources and systems of information, particularly in the eenvironment. Application of newer management concepts and techniques like 'TQM', 'Marketing', in not only identifying users and their exact needs but also in bringing
- delight to them by providing need-based services and products.
- Human resource issues vis-à-vis changing job requirements.

The International Federation of Library Associations and Institutions (IFLA), the American Library Association (ALA), the Library Association (LA), London and quite a few other similar level organisations are conducting CPDPs at international level. In the Indian context, the following bodies have taken praise-worthy initiatives in conducting CPDPs:

- National institutions - Defence Scientific Information and Documentation Centre (DESIDOC), National Social Science Documentation Centre (NASSDOC), National Medical Library (NML), All Indian Institute of Medical Sciences
- (AIIMS), National Information System for Science and Technology (NISSAT). Libraries at Indian Institutes of Management (IIMs), Indian Institute of Sciences
- (IISc), Indian Institutes of Technology (IITs), and some Central Universities. Professional associations - Indian Library Association (ILA), Indian Association of Special Libraries and Information Centres (IASLIC), Society for Information Systems (SIS), Indian Association of Teachers in Library and Information Science
- (IATLIS), Uttar Pradesh Library Association (UPLA). Library schools and training centres - all LIS Schools, National Institute of Science Communication and Information Resources (NISCAIR) - erstwhile Indian National Scientific and Documentation Centre (INSDOC) -, Documentation
- Research and Training Centre (DRTC).
- UGC - academic staff colleges of different universities, INFLIBNET.
- Consultants - retired people of the profession.
- Library networks - Delhi Library Network (DELNET), Ahmadabad Information Network (ADINET), Mysore Library Network (MYLIBNET), Pune Library Network (PUNENET), Bombay Library Network (BONET), Madras Library Network (MALIBNET), etc.

The Indian Institute of Management Lucknow (IIML) is a national level management institute set up by the Government of India. The mission of IIML is 'to help improve the management of the corporate and the non-corporate sectors and also the public systems, through pursuit of excellence in management education, research, consultancy, and training'. In keeping with the mission of the Institute, the library has been established "to facilitate knowledge generation and application through its effective dissemination". Besides catering to the diverse information needs of all its internal users, the library is offering its services, of course under specified terms and conditions, to the clientele in the external environment, as well.

Given the mission and vision of IIML and its library, the thinking that emerged at the Institute was that in the present context of knowledge-driven economy, organisations will excel in achieving their desired goals and objectives only if they are backed up by adequate information support systems. For that to happen, it was felt that these systems -the libraries and information centres (LICs) - needed to be managed well. It is basically in line with this thinking as well as with a view to equip these LICs with professionally competent librarians and information managers (LIMs) that IIML took upon itself the task of organising CPDPs for LIS professionals. The other reason responsible for IIML to take up this initiative was that an informal feedback about the programmes conducted by the other agencies, as outlined earlier, had revealed that programmes will have desired impact only if:

- conducted at such places that can provide the participants an opportunity of supplementing their theoretical insights/learning with practical experiences and skills in lab environment; and
- conducted by experts with sound knowledge in both theoretical as well as practical domains.

**Initiative by the Library at IIML**

Specifically mentioning about the driving force/s responsible for prompting the library to launch programmes in the area of 'quality management', it would be in order to state that the library having achieved the status of a national level learning resource center in the field of management and related areas - be in terms of its quality learning resources, or quality equipment and facilities put in place, or quality services it was rendering - it was time for the team at the library to share its rich experience with fellow professionals with a view to help them built 'quality' information support centers and systems for their respective organisations.

Since the library had right from its inception made extensive use of the state-of-the-art information technology offerings for all that it was doing for 'acquiring', 'organising' and 'disseminating' information for its highly demanding clientele, it had, over the years, gathered very enriching experiences as regards the application of IT in library environment. To share the same, the library thought of conducting CDPDs for fellow professionals, so that they don't indulge themselves in what is called as 'reinventing the wheel'. Similarly, to justify the conduct of CPDPs in the area of 'marketing', it will be apt to mention that the team and its management at the library had observed that the resources, facilities, and services developed at the library, over a period of time, were not being optimally utilised as long as their use was restricted to its primary members.

At the same time it was also felt that there was acute need of access to such learning resources, facilities, and services from a good number of users in the external environment. To address both these concerns, it was decided to experiment with bringing in 'marketing' orientation at the library itself. The experiment was successful in more ways than one. Not only did it help in enhancing the usage of the library but it also helped in satisfying the long felt need of external users. Added to both these advantages was the byproduct -some amount of revenue generation. However, all this did not happen over night. Rich experiences and learnings were there and it was felt that the same need to be shared among all those engaged in the information sector.

The library at IIML has already, conducted 27 CPDPs for LIS professionals in the area of 'Quality Management' ; 'Information Technology Applications'; and 'Marketing'. Besides, it also conducted some more CPDPs in other LIS areas and these include one programme each in the areas of 'Human Relations' and 'Effective Communication'. It is worthwhile to mention here that the author, on invitation, conducted a very successful programme on 'quality management and marketing' for 25 senior LIS professionals from Asian countries, in Singapore, during April 12-16, 1999 and he has since been a regular resource faculty for almost all the top level CPDPs for LIS professionals, conducted by various agencies in the country.

## CPDPs on 'Quality Management'

Library and Information Managers (LIM) are these days deluged with advice as to how to acquire and organise learning resources and satisfy the complex and ever increasing information needs of their users. However, to achieve their goal, the question of a resource constrained regime has to be kept in mind without sacrificing the interests of the users. The services offered, accordingly, have to be internally efficient and externally effective.

Programme Structure: Developing total quality management (TQM) as a strategic focus to effect continuous improvement in various activities and services of a modern library and information center(LIC) encompassing acquisition, organisation and

- dissemination of information.
- Understanding the TQM process. Barriers to continuous improvement in the context of library and information services (LIS).
- Making continuous improvement a way of life for everyone involved in LIS in any organisation

**CPDPs on 'Information Technology Applications'**

Information Technology (IT) has ushered in a variety of media that can help Library and Information Managers (LIMs) in efficient and effective acquisition, organisation and dissemination of information. Computers and CD ROMs have found increasing acceptance in Library & Information Centres (LICs); Multimedia has shown much potential for LICs; and Information Networks have broken time and space barriers. At the same time, LIMs are deluged with advice as to how to use this media to acquire and organise learning resources and satisfy the complex and ever increasing information needs of their users. In view of this and that of a resource constrained regime, LIMs will have to

- make right selections while choosing appropriate IT products and infrastructural facilities, (ii) understand the information seeking behaviour of users; and
- understand all policy and managerial issues in regard to the use of IT products.

Programme Structure:

- State-of-the-art IT application in LICs;
- Library Automation (in Integrated, Multiuser & Networked Environment);
- CD-ROM Databases/Networking & Online Document Access, Retrieval and Delivery;

- Networking & Internet (Protocols, DNS, Application in LICs);
- Preparing Website, Measuring & Improving its Efficiency; and
- Human Resource, Policy Considerations & Management Issues.

## CPDPs on 'Marketing'

Library and Information Centres (LICs) are now able to generate, by virtue of their using advanced computers and softwares, various kinds of information products and services in addition to their routine activities and services. However, it is a little unfortunate that these remain largely underutilised, or even, in cases, wholly unutilised. The reasons cited are several and include the following:

- Efforts in identifying and reaching out the target audience are inadequate. Information products and services are 'generator' driven rather than 'user' driven and in that there remains a "linkage gap" between the generators and
- users of such products and services; and Level and information awareness or consciousness is still low among the
- users and there is a need to raise it further.

An attempt is being made to equip the participants with adequate know how so that they are able to:

- Identify and understand their potential users (internal as well as-external) in relation to their resources and facilities;
- Understand the information needs of such users more accurately and precisely;

– Generate information products and services that are tailored to meet the exact needs of such users; and
– Remain cost-effective in the process of generating information products and services.

Broad Contents: The programme content, which kept on getting modified as well as updated from one programme to another, was largely designed around the following themes:

– understanding the marketing process;
– marketing in the library and information context;
– 4 Ps (Product, Price, Promotion and Distribution) of marketing in the context of information products and services;
– generating information products & services as sustainable sources of revenue generation; and
– Customer Relationship Marketing (CRM) Initiatives.

The contents for the first set of programme in each area were observed to be largely theory based with very little illustrations from the LIS world. Trying to make up for this deficiency in the subsequent programmes by introducing case method of teaching and learning, useful insight came through the 'feedback' that cases discussed be better from the library and information world. Having addressed all these concerns, one more useful insight came through the 'feedback' that the cases/case lets discussed be relevant to the Indian situation/context and that is where we have been trying to work on for our future programmes.

*Programme Schedule*: Final schedule for the three-day programme, as got evolved and fine-tuned on the basis of experience gained (and feedback provided by the participants as well as the resource faculty) in each area was worked out in such a manner that Day One was devoted to providing conceptual clarity on the 'subject' fundamentals, especially as related to their relevance in the library and information environment. Attempt, in Day One, was also made to orient the participants to 'case' method of learning.

Days Two and Three would, through case-study based approach, attempt at bringing out clarity on the application of 'subject concepts' in the context of library and information activities and services. The participants would then be, based on the SWOT analysis of their respective set-ups, advised to work out an action plan for their respective set-ups. The Action Plan would be firmed up under the guidance of the resource faculty towards the end of the Day Three and that would be the key take from the programme.

## Programme Delivery

All the technical sessions were handled by a faculty mix of experienced academics in the relevant subject area as well as practitioners in the field of LIS. Case study based approach was followed all through with examples and illustrations from the information world, both in Indian as well as foreign environment. Experience sharing sessions among the participants proved to be enriching component of the programmes as their active participation in the sessions, moderated by the Programme Director, provided very useful insights into their success as well as failure stories on the subject.

## Participant Profile

All programmes saw participation of nearly five hundred top and middle level qualified professionals, engaged in almost all the activities of a typical modern library and information centre, be in the area of acquisition, organisation, or services. Of course, some had also been involved in planning, designing, and developing the buildings and other infrastructure support for their library and information systems. It is worthwhile to mention here that the then INSDOC, DESIDOC, the British Council, the American Center, IITs, IISc, had been regularly sending their nominees to the programmes. Yes, the other participants to these programmes came from other academic institutions, government departments, research labs, industrial out-fits, but predominantly they were from scientific/industrial research and training institutions.

**Programme Feedback**

Going by the participants' feedback - summary of the latest programmes on 'quality management', 'information technology', and 'marketing' provided in Annexures 1 to 3, respectively - obtained from them with the help of a structured questionnaire, as well as through other formal (participants' reactions in the valedictory sessions) and informal modes (grape-vines, etc), the programmes were reported to have been very well received.

*Feedback Parameters*: Formal 'feedback' instrument administered to the participants at the end of the programme, was very useful in soliciting their pointed 'feedback' on a 5-point scale on following parameters:

- achievement of the course objectives, as mentioned in the announcement brochure/s;
- relevance and usefulness of the course to the participant's area of work;
- programme duration;
- programme contents;
- applicability of concepts discussed;
- conduct of the programme;
- programme design in terms of extent of coverage, conceptual clarity, orientation to practical problems, methodology;

- faculty mix;
- course material/lecture notes;
- interaction with fellow participants;
- extent of useful knowledge acquired from the course;
- any session found particularly useful or could have been dropped;
- training methodology in the context of presentations by the resource faculty, case preparation/discussion, group interaction;
- resource faculty assessment;
- hospitality in terms of boarding, lodging, transportation; and
- overall assessment of the course; and
- general comments and suggestions.

*Feedback Rating*: Generally speaking, almost all the programmes received, on an average, an overall feedback of +- 4.5 out of 5.

*Feedback Suggestions*: However, some of the specific suggestions that came from the feedback included the following:

- cases used be library and information specific;
- cases be situation specific in the Indian context; examples cited, to illustrate the 'concept/technique' application, be more
- oriented towards library and information world;
- duration of the programme be increased;
- more opportunity for sharing experiences among the participants should be provided;
- a proper balance in resource faculty between academics and practitioners not only in the LIS but other area/s

(depending upon the theme of the programme) be maintained; and

– adequate time, may be beyond regular programme hours, may be made available to the participants to facilitate their study of the growth, development and management of the IIML library itself, with specific focus on the area of programme.

All these useful inputs and many more were duly taken note of and needful done as appropriate in the subsequent programmes. Some other positive comments were "very useful programme in the present context"; "right step in right direction at right time"; "case orientation towards librarianship" very useful; and so on.

10

# Lifestyle Related Diseases

Global Campaign for Education suggests that if all children received a complete primary education, the economic impact of HIV/AIDS could be greatly reduced and around 700,000 cases of HIV in young adults could be prevented each year - 7 million in a decade. HIV/AIDS is spreading fastest among young women (ages 15-24), not only because their physiology puts them at risk, but also because they have little access to knowledge, economic resources and decision-making power. Education changes this equation, giving women the information and the clout they need to keep themselves safe.

Literate women are three times more likely than illiterate women to know that a healthy-looking person can have HIV, and four times more likely to know the main ways to avoid AIDS, according to a 32-country UN study. Evidence from 17 countries in Africa and four in Latin America shows that bettereducated girls hold off longer on sexual activity, and are more likely to require their partners to use condoms. Women with some schooling are nearly five times as likely as uneducated women to have used a condom the last time they had sex. But education also accelerates behaviour change among young men, making them more receptive to prevention messages and more likely to adopt condom use.

Education is so strongly predictive of better knowledge, safer behaviour and reduced infection rates that it has been described as the "social vaccine", and UN and World Bank experts say it may be 'the single most effective preventive weapon against HIV/AIDS'. Andin countries with high or fast-growing prevalence rates, getting every child into school now is essential to stop AIDS destroying the fragile stock of human capital on which poor people's livelihoods -and developing countries' economic futures - depend. Whereas experts postulate that economic growth in countries hard-hit by HIV/AIDS will drop by 1-4 per cent a year, UN research suggests that raising the average education of the labour force by one year raises GDP by 9 per cent. Each year of basic education, the 'people's asset', increases the productivity of African peasant farmers by 3-14 per cent.

Despite the proven efficacy of education in fighting the onslaught of HIV, over 100 million children worldwide are still missing school. Rich countries are not delivering the promised aid and debt relief that developing countries need to hire more teachers and build more classrooms. Without urgent action, including substantial increases in aid to education, Africa will not be able to get every child into school for another 150 years. For relatively small amounts of money, donors could ensure that every girl and every boy receives a quality basic education. An additional US$5.6 billion in aid to basic education, intelligently targeted via the Education for All Fast Track Initiative, would dramatically increase our chances of halting and reversing the HIV/AIDS epidemic in the next decade.

Universal primary education is not a substitute for expanded HIV/AIDS treatment and prevention. Both are complementary; and both are urgently necessary if we are to win the fight against the disease. To achieve UPE, halt and reverse HIV/AIDS, and fulfill the other UN development goals, overall aid budgets must rise to at least

0.7 per cent of GNI in line with the commitments made in Monterrey. At least 10 per cent of that should be devoted to basic education. In addition, about US$10bn annually will be required to mount adequate treatment and prevention programmes in all developing countries, including an estimated US$7bn to underwrite the Global Fund to Fight AIDS, Tuberculosis and Malaria.

The combined annual cost of UPE and expanded treatment and prevention - US$16bn - is less than the amount Europeans and Americans spend on pet food every year. In the words of Angeline Mugwendere, leader of an African youth network, 'Education is a lethal blow to AIDS. With access to school, many of my friends would be alive today.' The World Bank Spring Meetings in April 2004 provide an opportunity for rich countries to start making a difference now by properly funding and coordinating the Education for All effort:

- Increases in aid to education must reach the countries that have greatest need of additional resources, and have shown the strongest commitment to achieving Education for All. Finance and development ministers should strengthen and expand the Fast Track Initiative to serve as the coordinating mechanism through which donors will identify and collectively support the countries whose funding needs deserve the highest priority. Fast Track partners should pledge to channel 75 per cent of new aid for basic education to Fast Track-endorsed countries.
- As a first step, rich countries must immediately make up the remaining funding shortfalls for the 12 low-income countries whose education plans they have already endorsed through the Education for All Fast Track Initiative.
- Finance and development ministers meeting in Washington this week should call for a review of the 34 additional countries that have already qualified for Fast

Track status, but have not yet had plans endorsed. The review should establish whether the country is in possession of a credible plan for achieving Education for All (EFA), whether existing donor commitments are adequate to support this plan, and whether outstanding finance needs can be met through existing in-country channels. Findings should be presented to the Fast Track partnership and the Development Committee in Spring 2005.

– Beyond this, rich countries must begin to work with developing countries in genuine partnership. Key markers of this would be the inclusion of Southern ministers on the steering committee of the Education for All Fast Track Initiative, an end to donoronly meetings, and full implementation of a transparent system to monitor the quality as well as the quantity of donor aid to education.

– Finance ministers of developing countries should ensure that they are increasing budgets for basic education alongside budgets for primary health care and AIDS prevention and care. Priorities for increased education spending should include abolishing primary school fees and charges; achieving gender parity in both primary and secondary education; improving teacher training; and incorporating sexual and reproductive health education and life skills training into the curriculum.

As Nelson Mandela has noted, 'Education is the most powerful weapon you can use to change the world.' It is also a weapon that the world cannot do without in the fight against HIV/AIDS. Education saves lives. And ignorance is lethal.

## HIV/AIDS and the "Education Vaccine"

HIV/AIDS is killing millions of people worldwide. On current trends, another 5 million people will contract HIV each year. Of these, nearly half will be 15-24-year-olds in the lowincome countries - the overwhelming majority of them girls and young women. Recognising that young people hold the key to stopping AIDS, at the UN General Assembly Special Session on AIDS world leaders committed to reduce HIV prevalence among 15-24-year-olds by 25 per cent by the year 2010. Yet prevalence is still on the rise in this age group, and as long as this remains the case, the epidemic will continue to grow. The causal factors are complex and there is no single intervention or policy that can protect everyone at risk.

But 700,000 cases of HIV would be prevented each year if all children received a complete primary education. Education is so strongly predictive of better knowledge, safer behaviour and reduced infection rates that UN experts conclude education functions as a kind of "social vaccine". Recent studies indicate that young people with little or no education may be 2.2 times more likely to contract HIV as those who have completed primary education. This implies that, while those without a complete primary education represent around 36 per cent of young adults in low-income countries, they are likely to experience around 55 per cent of new HIV cases for that age group. Without universal primary education (UPE), we can expect 1.3 million young adults who lack primary education to become infected every year - a substantial proportion of the predicted 5 million new infections annually.

However, if everyone received a full primary education, we would expect over 700,000 of these cases (about 30 per cent of all new infections in this age group) to be prevented each year. These figures are only broad estimates, based on the limited data that is currently available. Evidence from around the world suggests that many more could be saved if HIV prevention was mainstreamed in schools, and universal primary completion was used to underpin an expanded prevention strategy. But even allowing for the difficulty of obtaining precise figures, it is clear that the continuing failure to provide all children with at least a primary education is leaving millions unprotected from infection and leading to chronic levels of avoidable suffering. It is literally a fatal mistake.

Alongside UPE and other prevention measures, there would still be an urgent and compelling need for expanded treatment, care and support for those infected. Only through comprehensive treatment measures, including anti-retroviral drugs, and universal education, can we stave off the insidious downward spiral of impoverishment and deskilling that may yet be the epidemic's deadliest long-term legacy.

AIDS does more than destroy the knowledge and skills of those who die from it. 'It also deprives their children of those very things they need to become economically productive adults - their parents' loving care, knowledge and capacity to finance education.' The erosion of human and social capital is gradual but relentless; enough, they argue, to lead hard-hit countries to the brink of economic and social collapse within a few decades. "AIDS is more devastating than any terrorist attack, any conflict, or any weapon of mass destruction". By helping families keep children in school - through investing in steps such as making education free, expanding the number of classrooms and teachers, and providing additional incentives to poor parents - developing countries, supported by international donors, can protect and even strengthen the base of skills and knowledge that is the main foundation of economic growth.

Education has been described as 'the people's asset', crucial to enable those who are most likely to be poor - girls, ethnic minorities, orphans, people with disabilities, those living in rural areas - to contribute to and benefit from economic growth. Each year of schooling increases individual productivity, and hence income, by about 3-14 per cent. Finally, investing in the 'education vaccine' would yield other well-documented economic and social benefits. It would free up badly-needed health sector resources, as the total costs of keeping a child in school for six to nine years are likely to be far less than the lifetime costs of caring for her, and possibly her infected or orphaned children, should she become HIV positive. Moreover, those saved from infection through schooling would also escape the crippling costs associated with sickness, lost work days and early death - which have been shown to reduce a family's lifetime income by as much as 48 per cent.

Whether or not individuals contract HIV, education will boost their earning power, as argued above, and their children's chances of a healthy and prosperous life. Mothers with even a few years of education are better able to ensure that their children grow up healthy, well-fed and educated - hence, less likely to become infected themselves. As Kofi Annan has said of girls' education: "No other policy is as likely to raise economic productivity, lower infant and maternal mortality, improve nutrition and promote health."

Good quality education is in itself a powerful weapon against HIV/AIDs. 'It is mainly women excluded from education who fall prey to this disease. The role of education in reducing HIV prevalence amongst young adults cannot be explained by exposure to specific HIV prevention classes, as very few of those tested would have been at school when such classes were first introduced. Rather, it is general schooling that appears to make the most powerful impact on young people's sexual behaviour and choices. A complete primary education leads to increased ability to evaluate, understand and apply facts; gains in confidence; and greater decisionmaking power in relationships. It creates the context in which preventative messages about HIV can best be understood and acted upon.

Education is especially empowering for girls and young women, and this is key to its efficacy against HIV/

AIDS, a disease which thrives on the social and economic vulnerability of young women. Globally, about one-third of those currently living with HIV/AIDS are aged 15-24 and the majority of new infections also occur among young adults. Adolescent girls are the single most affected segment of the population. In Sub-Saharan Africa, more than two-thirds of newly infected 15-19-year-olds are female and over 8 per cent of young women are currently living with HIV/AIDS, compared with around 4 per cent of young men. In the most devastated countries, the rate of new HIV infections among girls is five to six times higher than for boys. Young women's vulnerability to AIDS is not just physiological; more fundamentally, it is a result of women's disempowerment.

As the World Association of Girl Guides and Girl Scouts and VSO point out, gender inequality keeps women economically dependent; makes it difficult for them to mention, let alone practise, safe sex; subjects them to sexual violence; and, once infected, pushes them to the end of the treatment queue. The same gender inequality is what currently deprives 67 million girls of schooling and keeps 553 million women illiterate. Reversing economic and cultural discrimination against women requires structural changes that can take decades, but getting girls into school offers a clear start along this road. And new research shows that it makes an enormous contribution to efforts to reduce the spread of HIV.

Literate women are three times more likely than illiterate women to know that a healthylooking person can have HIV, and four times more likely to know the main ways to avoid AIDS, according to a 32-country study. Although knowledge levels are predictably greatest among women with secondary or better education, primary education in itself makes a very significant impact. Analysing data from UNICEF's Multi-Indicator Cluster Survey for 12 countries, we found that women with a primary education were 2.5 times more likely than women with no schooling to correctly identify the main ways to prevent HIV transmission.

Among rural women, who have less access to media and information than urban women, the effects of primary education on HIV knowledge were even greater. significant impact. Analysing data from UNICEF's Multi-Indicator Cluster Survey for 12 countries, found that women with a primary education were 2.5 times more likely than women with no schooling to correctly identify the main ways to prevent HIV transmission. Among rural women, who have less access to media and information than urban women, the effects of primary education on HIV knowledge were even greater. But education does more than give girls, and boys, access to facts; it also increases their confidence and power in society, so that they are in a better position to act on what they know.

The empowering effects of education reach into nearly all choices and relationships that statisticians have found ways to measure, from the number of children women have to whether or not they control their own income. Not surprisingly, then, education has also been shown to provide girls and women with a better negotiating position to avoid unwanted sexual intercourse and to insist on condom use, whilst also making young men more receptive to condom promotion messages. Evidence from 17 countries in Africa and four in Latin America shows that better-educated girls hold off longer on sexual activity, and are more likely to require their partners to use condoms.

Recent household surveys in 11 countries show that women with some schooling were nearly five times as likely as uneducated women to have used a condom the last time they had sex. The effects of education on reported condom use are equally striking for young men. In the past five to ten years, since the risks of HIV infection in developing countries have been recognised, better educated young people have increased condom use and reduced the number of casual partners at a much steeper rate than those with little or no education. During the 1990s the HIV infection rate fell by almost half among educated women, but there was little decline for women without any formal schooling.

Girls of a similar age who had dropped out of school were more than six times more likely to be HIV-positive. What is more, young women with secondary education remained less vulnerable to HIV for years after they left school. By contrast, unequal access to education for women is correlated with higher infection rates among all adults, men as well as women. A study in 72 capital cities found significantly higher infection rates where the literacy gap between women and men was larger. According to another study, countries where the literacy gap between boys and girls is above 25 per cent were more likely to reach the commonly cited 'outbreak' level of 5 per cent HIV prevalence. Lack of education, particularly among girls and women, may also help to speed the spread of AIDS by reducing general levels of health and nutrition.

Children born to uneducated mothers are more likely to be malnourished, less likely to be immunised, and have lower average height, a strong indicator of poor health. Education helps girls gain the clout and the standing in society to avoid high-risk behaviours and save their own lives. Education not only helps individuals to protect themselves against HIV but also helps societies as a whole to work together to keep people safe. Universalising education, and including life skills and sexual and reproductive health within the UPE curriculum, is particularly important in this regard.

As the World Bank points out, societies with better levels of education across the population are better and faster at creating, applying and spreading new ideas and information. The silence and stigma that hold back individuals from accessing preventative services and advice are exacerbated not only by the lack of education of those individuals, but by lack of education amongst the communities in which they live. Escaping taboos requires collective social change. To date, no medical vaccine has been discovered for HIV. The education vaccine is not only the best one available, but is also, as UNICEF notes, 'likely to be the only one available for the foreseeable future.'

School-based HIV/AIDS Education can enhance the impact of universal primary completion: The general cognitive and social gains from a basic education are the most important factor in protecting adolescents and young adults from infection. But schools also provide a crucial opportunity to reach children with prevention messages before they become sexually active, and if this opportunity is seized through well-designed sexual and reproductive health education programmes, the protective impact of schooling can be considerably enhanced. Schools, as the World Bank points out, 'offer an organised and efficient way to reach large numbers of school-age youth' at an age when they are highly receptive to adult influence.

In fact, a recent systematic review found stronger evidence for the efficacy of school-based programmes than for any other prevention measure. School-based interventions had a clearer impact on age at first sex and number of sexual partners than any other measure; and they had an equally strong impact on condom use as peer counselling, workplace education and voluntary testing and counselling. Similarly, a review of 113 studies from 5 continents found that school-based AIDS education that focus on specific age-appropriate behavioral objectives are effective in reducing early sexual activity and high-risk behavior.

Information received in the classroom is especially important to girls, who are far less likely than boys to have basic knowledge about how to protect themselves from HIV/AIDS and have less access to other sources of accurate information, as explained by one young girl from Chennai, India:

> 'Children get most of their information from school. This is especially true with girls, as we remain confined to the home outside school hours. Boys have the freedom to go out with their friends, to the movies etc., so they have a better chance of getting additional information. As girls, after a certain age we stay at home and only go out to study. School is therefore the basic source for girls.

Yet a recent worldwide study found that about 40 per cent of countries have not yet taken the basic step of including AIDS in their school curriculum. And even where school-based programmes have been developed, not all of them have been effective. Most importantly, school-based programmes will work best when the school itself is working properly. Effective AIDS education demands that policy-makers address the wider quality challenges facing schools, and tackle problems such as class sizes of 60 or more; absence of books and chalk; students who arrive too hungry to concentrate; overworked, under-trained and underpaid teachers; and lack of community involvement in school affairs. Secondly, the chances of success are slim unless teachers are involved in designing schoolbased preventative classes, and receive specific training and support to implement them.

Frank discussions of sexual issues in the classroom may be impossible in such circumstances. Through a unique programme initiated by Education International and the World Health Organisation, teachers' unions in 17 countries are working hand in hand with ministries of education and health to train thousands of teachers on the life skills needed to prevent HIV/AIDS. The programme has increased teachers' confidence in discussing HIV/AIDS issues in a school setting and has helped to break down the 'walls of silence' surrounding HIV. Building links between what happens in the classroom and what happens in the community can improve results. The Ghana Education Service's Girls Education Unit has launched a programme to improve the capacity of 11- to 15-year-old girls to protect themselves from HIV infection.

The campaign targets all primary and junior secondary schools in Ghana but also addresses child welfare NGOs operating at the community level, as well as boys, teachers, parents, and community members. In Congo, Tanzania, Nigeria and other countries, successful projects have trained students to act as peer educators outside the classroom, and groups like the Forum of African Women Educationalists (FAWE) and the Girl Guides use after-school clubs and activities to combat stigma and promote awareness.

In addition to ensuring access to education, key aspects of any successful strategy include:

– Providing meaningful information to enable people to know how best to protect themselves from HIV/AIDS and how they can get support;

– Providing condoms, HIV counselling and testing, and treatment of sexually transmitted infections, and ensuring that services are properly accessible;

– Developing a political, media and public culture in which issues surrounding HIV/AIDS can be discussed in an open and non-stigmatising way, and challenging prejudice and discrimination;

– Increasing the constructive involvement of men and boys in activities designed to reduce gender inequality and prevent the spread of HIV/AIDS;

– Providing real social and economic opportunities so that people can choose safer life strategies;

– Ensuring that the 'hardest to reach' groups are included in all HIV prevention work - as they are often the people most at risk.

Each of these measures is mutually reinforcing. Crucially, all of them rest in large part on the provision of universal education. Without education, young people - especially girls, and those from 'hardest to reach' groups - are less likely to understand the information provided; less confident in accessing services; less likely to be able to discuss HIV issues openly and without stigma; and less likely to have real social and economic opportunities. Higher levels of education have also been shown to increase women's ability to seek and receive medical treatment for themselves. As UNICEF concluded, 'The four allies that make the virus so prevalent in many developing countries are silence, shame, stigma and superstition. These all thrive in a climate of ignorance and illiteracy.'

More teachers must be trained to replace those lost to AIDS, and better ways to support HIV-positive teachers are needed. Improving teacher training, motivation and morale is also essential to the success of school-based prevention programmes. Expand universal education beyond primary level, with a particular focus on increasing opportunities for women and girls. Once children have a primary education, the benefits to society and to individuals increase even further if they can complete a secondary education as well. Unfortunately, in many developing countries secondary schools are still the preserve of an affluent and largely male minority. Getting all children through primary school is a necessary first step towards equitable access to secondary and further education.

However, to unlock the full economic and social impact of universal education, an important next step is extend free and compulsory schooling to at least age 15. What is more, among the 15-24 age group most at risk of HIV infection in the developing world, one in three have already dropped out of school without basic literacy skills, and are therefore doubly at risk from HIV. Adult literacy classes and non-formal education programmes are needed to reach this critical segment of the population with information and skills that could save their lives. Mainstream life skills and sexual and reproductive health education in the primary and secondary curriculum and upgrade teacher training to ensure that teachers can teach these topics effectively. Take further steps to ensure that schools are empowering, positive and safe environments for girls.

Of course, all of these measures require good planning and political will, but they are also all impossible without increased resources from developing country governments themselves, and from rich countries. UNESCO estimates the additional external funding required to achieve universal primary education at US$5.6 billion a year, of which some US$550 million per year represents the costs of coping with HIV/AIDS (mainly additional teacher training and recruitment, as well as targeted subsidies to AIDS orphans). To put this figure into perspective, it is:

- Less than a third of global annual spending on video games;
- Less than one-tenth of the cost of the invasion of Iraq;
- Less than 0.03 per cent of donor countries' combined annual gross national income.

World leaders meeting in Dakar in 2000 pledged that no developing country seriously committed to education for all would be denied the external resources necessary to achieve it. However, international funding provided for Education For All has remained woefully inadequate. Of the US$7 billion required annually from rich countries for UPE, only US$1.4 billion is being provided. Only the Netherlands and Luxembourg are providing their fair share of the funding required, with the USA, Germany, and Japan amongst the worst laggards, needing to increase their aid to basic education by at least 10 times.

Warped geographical distribution of aid means that those countries with the greatest need do not receive their fair share of even that meagre support. Much too little of the aid for education is provided to where the largest number of out-of-school children live. South and West Asia and Sub-Saharan Africa, which together hold 73 per cent of the world's out-ofschool children, receive just 36 per cent of the education aid. And key G7 countries USA, Japan, and France still provide only half of their aid to poor countries, with the other half spent on middle-income allies.

Finally, much aid to education remains highly ineffective because it is too short-term or too restricted to allow countries to plan comprehensive action on the EFA goals. Lack of predictable and coordinated donor funding for recurrent costs remains a major barrier. A major step towards more effective donor support to EFA was taken at the World Bank Spring Meetings in 2002, with the launch of the Education for All Fast Track Initiative (FTI).

For the first time, the FTI establishes clear and transparent criteria, agreed by all donors, for identifying the countries which both need additional resources and have put in place the policies needed to use those resources most effectively. Many of the first 18 countries invited to join the FTI have already committed to far-reaching and ambitious reform of their education systems in order to get every child into school. The first 10 FTI countries to receive donor endorsement for their plans have been raising enrolments and primary school completion at a rate many times faster than other developing countries, and with more aid, they could achieve even more. By using the FTI process to make decisions about how to allocate all of their aid to education, donors could target their resources where they will make the greatest impact.

But most donors are putting only a tiny fraction of their aid budgets into new resources for FTIapproved plans. As new figures show, far from being rewarded for good performance, not one of the first 12 countries endorsed by international donors for the FTI has been provided with the funding required for even the next two years - and funding is even more uncertain after that.

Even the official "progress report", prepared by the FTI secretariat for the Development Committee meeting in Washington this week, admits that the funding so far provided "falls far short of the level required" and notes that the prospects of achieving education for all "are dim unless there is a substantial improvement in international response". This represents a missed opportunity that is not only shameful, but in the context of AIDS, totally inexcusable. Donors could make an immediate difference to the future of over three million out-of-school children in the first 12 FTI countries by finding the extra funds needed to fully back their EFA strategies. That, however, is only the start of the story. By increasing budgets for aid to education, and targeting these increased resources to countries collectively endorsed by donors through the FTI process, donors would be working together to create powerful incentives for all developing countries to scale up their education efforts - our best chance of helping all the world's 100 million out-of-school children.

# 11

# The Consequences of Global Educational Expansion

Human capital stock is central to national economic development, as better-educated citizens are more productive. There is an obvious coincidence of educational expansion and national economic development: developed countries tend to have more educated populations than less-developed countries.

The impact of government policies on long-run growth concludes that the most definitive results relate to the positive impact of education expenditures: eleven of the twelve empirical studies identified showed significant, positive effects of educational expenditures on growth. A long-term positive effect of educational expenditures on economic growth. On the other hand, associations between measures of educational expansion and indicators of economic growth are open to interpretation.

The best way to isolate causal impacts on national development. Two factors contribute to the controversy: the difficulty of distinguishing the effects of growth on education from the effects of education on growth, and the possibility that other factors drive both educational expansion and economic growth. One possible explanation for controversies surrounding the educationgrowth relationship is a mismatch between education and labor market demands in some countries. In settings where the formal sector is poorly developed, education may be seen as filling slots in the labor market, rather than helping individuals create new opportunities in the market. To the extent that labor markets are static in this way, the incidence of unemployment may rise with education and increases in education may reduce total output.

The relationship between education and economic development to data problems such as measurement error and time-frame limitations. There is considerable measurement error in country-level education data, particularly at secondary and tertiary levels. After accounting for measurement error, they find that an increase in years of schooling has little short-term effect on GDP growth, but a positive and statistically significant effect on economic growth over periods of ten to twenty years. A third possible explanation for mixed results is that different levels of schooling may not have consistent consequences for growth across countries.

The levels of education that matter for economic development may depend on the nations' level of development: in less developed countries, primary and secondary education may matter more; in more developed countries, tertiary education may matter more. As globalization and technological change modify the imperative for education. Using an index of technological progress constructed of five components. Human capital investment is positively related to national technological progress.

There may be particular synergies between technology and human capital, and that high levels of education may be a necessary condition for technological innovation and adaptation. Only tertiary gross enrollment ratios are significantly positively linked to Internet use. In fact, controlling for tertiary enrollment ratios, secondary enrollment ratios are significantly negatively related to Internet use.

## Education and Individual Economic Welfare

Within societies, the expansion of educational opportunities enables individuals to improve their economic circumstances. The supposition that nations with more educated individuals should prosper hinges on the notion that better educated individuals are socialized in ways that increase their productivity and improve their economic standing. Sociology and economics have thoroughly investigated these assumptions. Sociologists have examined patterns and trends in individuals' school-to-work transitions and occupational attainment.

Whether education enables individuals to find better jobs and improve their economic status varies across industrialized and industrializing countries. Similarly, in the field of economics, studies show dramatic variations in the rates of return on investments in education across countries, as well as within countries across levels of schooling, social groups, and time periods.

Variations notwithstanding, these studies attest to the importance of education as a determinant of individuals' occupational outcomes and subsequent economic status. One concern about results such as these, however, is raised by the credentialism hypothesis. This hypothesis holds that education signals individuals who are privileged or talented, providing a convenient "job queue" for employers, rather than actually improving the productivity of indisviduals.

But empirical evidence casts doubt on such strict credentialist arguments. Further, in less-developed settings, educational expansion, particularly among women, also appears to have significant implications for the human capital of children of the newly-educated. A component of the significant positive relationship between maternal literacy and child schooling in India reflects the productivity effect of home teaching. This effect, combined with the increase in returns to schooling for men, underlies the expansion of female literacy following the onset of the green revolution.

The mechanisms underlying such findings are illuminated in anthropological studies in developing countries. Education helps women acquire aspirations, skills, and models of learning that eventually affect their child-bearing and child-rearing behaviors. The benefits of increased schooling for economic outcomes of individuals, and to the likely echo effects on their children. Yet, forecasting the specific economic implications of rising educational attainments is extremely complex, absent access to unusual data sources such as, for example, those on school construction utilized.

The difficulty is that individuals' economic opportunities are linked not only to their own human capital, but also to larger structural constraints. One complicating structural factor is that the poor, whose children are most likely to be out of school, are increasingly concentrated among social groups whose opportunities to translate schooling into productive activities may be very different from those of groups already reached by the school system. Children in impoverished and isolated areas often lack ready access to urban labor markets in which educational credentials directly affect employment.

The link between education and economic welfare for those remaining outside of the school system may be different, on average, than for those already in the school system. A second important structural constraint is that the value of an individual's own educational credential depends in part on how it compares to the credentials of others in the local population or labor market. As the average level of schooling in the population increases, the value of an individual's given level of education in the labor market declines. This phenomenon is termed "credential inflation."

In some countries, education is valued for the specific vocational skills it confers; in others, for providing workers with general knowledge; in others still, for sorting students by scholastic ability or potential to learn. Where education's main purpose is to sort students, there is a built-in incentive for young people to acquire more education in order to stay ahead of the queue. As ever-larger proportions of a population obtain a credential, its labor market value declines. In contrast, in countries where vocational qualifications are used by employers to organize jobs and allocate persons among them, the value of a credential derives not from its scarcity, but rather from the specific skills it represents.

**Social Inequalities**

Educational expansion narrows social inequalities within countries by promoting a meritocratic basis for status attainment. Structural constraints acknowledged, a convergence of evidence suggests that education plays an important role in improving the absolute economic standing of individuals. Whether educational expansion improves the relative standing of historically disadvantaged groups such as the poor, ethnic minorities, and women is a different question.

This "industrialism hypothesis" holds that as societies develop, urbanization, mass communication, and industrialization should lead to greater social openness and a shift from particularistic to universalistic bases of achievement. These changes, in turn, should tighten the link between education and economic mobility. Data constraints have precluded systematic evaluation of the industrialism hypothesis, but existing studies show only mixed support for the notion that development and educational expansion bring increased social mobility.

Educational expansion does not reduce the relative advantages of elite children over children from less-privileged backgrounds. Educational expansion alone does not change the relative position of social groups in the "education queue," and elites manage to maintain their status by getting more education than the masses. A wide range of societies finds little change in educational opportunities between social strata over the course of educational expansion. These findings highlight the need to consider separately the effects on educational opportunity of an increase in the overall size of the educational system and changes in the rules by which educational opportunities are allocated.

Even expansions in education accompanied by reforms designed to modify the allocation of educational opportunities within society do not always reduce educational inequality. A process of "maximally maintained inequality" explains why many sweeping reforms intended to make education more egalitarian have not accomplished their purpose. When advantaged groups are not fully integrated at a given level of education, they strongly support efforts to expand educational participation by eliminating tuition fees and increasing capacity.

Expansion at these levels of education does not lead to greater equality between social groups because advantaged groups, who tend to favor education, can garner the largest share of valuable educational credentials. In such cases, expansion does not alter the effect of social background on educational transitions. Furthermore, elite groups are well-positioned to see that their children are channeled into higher quality educational experiences, even within given levels of schooling.

### *Gender Inequality*

Evidence from countries around the world indicates a global, long-term trend toward equalization of the allocation of schooling between girls and boys. Nonetheless, there are some important caveats to this generalization. Sometimes, the persistence of gender gaps is linked to cultural norms surrounding women's roles in society, particularly women's access to paid employment. Norms of female participation in the labor-force can also condition the consequences of educational expansion among girls. Reduced gender disparities in education are not always mirrored by reduced gender gaps in employment and income.

### *Ethnic Inequality*

Because of the close link between education and occupational outcomes, increased absolute levels of education are likely to benefit disadvantaged ethnic groups. However, it is not safe to assume that expansion in access to education will allow disadvantaged minorities to "catch up" with initially advantaged ethnic groups, at least in the short run. Educational expansion across ethnic groups in recent decades has not led to substantial narrowing in educational disparities across these groups.

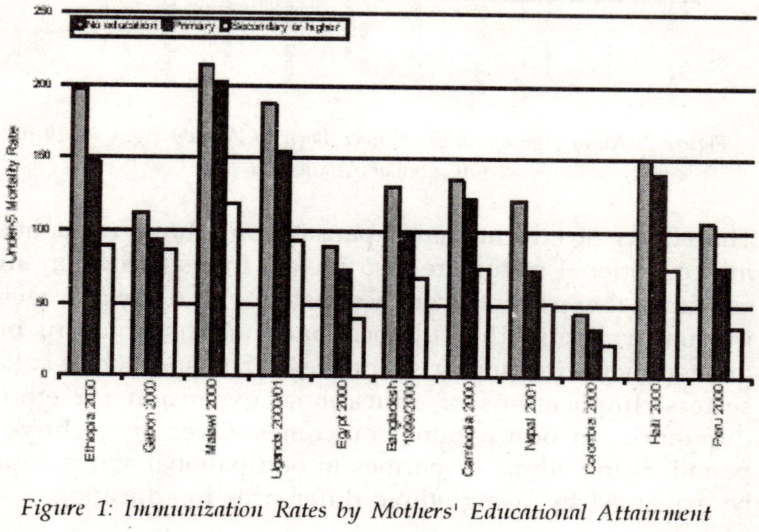


*Figure 1: Immunization Rates by Mothers' Educational Attainment*

Instead, patterns of access to formal education have closely mirrored traditional caste-ethnic hierarchies. The effects of ethnicity declined for the transition from primary to secondary schooling but remained constant for subsequent educational transitions. Considerable ethnic disparities persisted through the early 1990s, with progress toward equity at the stage of primary entrance offset by increasing disparities at the junior high-school stage.

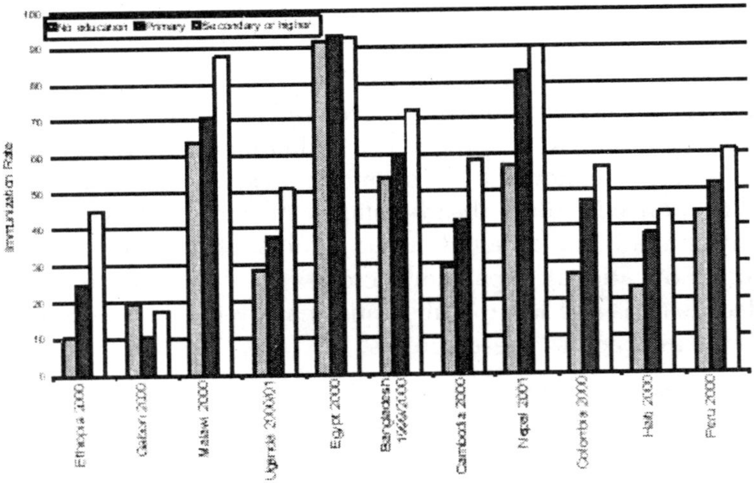


*Figure 2: Mean Age of Children Ever Born to Women Ages 40-49 by Educational Attainment*

The effects of educational expansion on ethnic inequalities in occupational status are also mixed. Industrialization and educational expansion were associated with decreased racial inequality across the full occupational distribution, but greater racial inequality in pro-fessional and white-collar sectors. Implications of educational expansion for ethnic differences in occupational outcomes. Over an eight-year period, rising ethnic disparities in occupational status could be explained by rising ethnic differences in education.

These educational disparities emerged at a time of dramatic improvements in access to schooling for both minorities and ethnic Chinese. Similarly despite educational expansion, educational disparities played an important role in maintaining race-based differences in occupational status in the 1980s and 1990s. In short, while educational expansion offers new economic opportunities to both advantaged and disadvantaged groups, its implications for reducing inequality associated with socioeconomic status, gender, and ethnicity are decidedly mixed.

While human capital disparities can be an important cause of occupational and income disparities across social groups, there are often important structural causes as well. As education becomes more central to occupations and incomes, those who are otherwise able but lack appropriate credentials are excluded, while those who gain credentials later may have a harder time converting credentials into high-status or high-wage employment. However, to maintain a balanced perspective on these findings, it is important to bear in mind that continued relative deprivation loses some of its significance if absolute deprivation is eased significantly by educational expansion.

## Education and Health

Countries with better-educated citizens have healthier populations, as educated individuals make more informed health choices, live longer, and have healthier children. There is evidence of important linkages between education and health. The education of children, especially girls, is associated with significantly longer life expectancies and lower death rates. Similarly, increases in enrollment ratios at all levels are associated with significant reductions in infant mortality per 1,000 live births. More educated individuals live longer and healthier lives. The mechanisms determining this relationship are complex.

In developing countries mechanisms linking women's education to infant and child health. Women with more education are more empowered to process information about health and negotiate better health care. Compared to uneducated mothers, educated mothers are more informed about preventive health-care practices such as immunizations; have greater decision-making power in health; are less fatalistic about disease; and are more likely to adopt innovative behaviors related to children's health. While these graphs only present bivariate relationships, the relationship between maternal education and child health appears across empirical studies that employ controls for other dimensions of socioeconomic status.

The populations of countries with more educated people grow more slowly, as educated citizens are able to implement a virtuous cycle of having fewer children. The association between education and fertility is well established. The average number of children born to women ages 40-49 by educational attainment. These graphs show a dominant pattern in which women with education, and especially secondary and higher education, tend to have substantially fewer children by the end of their childbearing years. The negative relationship between education, particularly secondary education, and fertility is also evident in national aggregate data. A higher infant survival rate may also extend the period of lactation and postpartum infecundability, thus reducing the time women are at risk of conceiving additional children.

Second, education encourages a later age at marriage. This effect emerges not only through direct competition between enrollment in school and marriage. Age at marriage was four years later for women with at least seven years of education than for uneducated women. Women's schooling had a strong effect on the timing of family formation, with the largest effect at the secondary level. Delaying marriage carries significant potential for reducing population growth, even in the absence of motivation for reducing family size.

Later marriage typically increases the mean length of a generation, or the time a cohort takes to replace itself, and thus slows population growth even at constant fertility levels. Third, in cases where women have more opportunities to engage in higher-status, better-paying jobs, the opportunity costs associated with childbearing and childrearing rise, and the time available for parenting decreases. Because access to non-familial employment expands with higher levels of education, better-educated women are more likely to delay or eschew childbearing. Moreover, with education and labor-force participation, women's status and decision-making authority may increase. This change relates to fertility in two ways.

Women's increased decision-making authority is associated with greater utilization of health resources and improved child health. Improved child health, in turn, provides the basis for limiting fertility. Also with increased decisionmaking authority, women are better able to implement fertility preferences. Better-educated women were more likely to use contraceptives. The onset of mass education, defined as the point at which 75 percent of 15-19 year-olds completed at least four grades of school, was linked to increased contraceptive practice.

A fourth route of education's influence on fertility lies in the effects of children's education on household structures and subsequent parental decisions about fertility. Several mechanisms by which children's schooling affects the household economy. Education creates a dependency of children upon parents. Rather than all family members contributing to the family economy, parents become responsible for supporting children for longer periods of time. Education increases the direct costs of raising children through school costs and increased pressures on parents to invest in their children.

Education reduces a child's availability for working inside and outside the home. For all of these reasons, educational expansion may reduce fertility by reducing the economic benefits and increasing the perceived costs associated with childbearing. New values might include occupational aspirations beyond the household and increasingly individually-oriented rather than family-oriented goals. Even the values of individuals who do not themselves attend school may be modified.

Childhood proximity to schools dramatically increased women's contraceptive use in adulthood: women who lived near a school during their childhood had a 39 percent higher annual odds of adopting a permanent contraceptive method, given that they had not already done so. This finding was largely independent of whether the woman subsequently attended school, her husband attended school, she lived near a school in adulthood, or she sent her children to school.

Together, the many pieces of evidence linking education to differences in fertility lead to the expectation that educational expansion contributes to long-term favorable demographic changes and, ultimately, slowed population growth. The significance of links between education and demographic change by including fertility and mortality differences by education in their population projections. The authors conclude that under the conditions of large age differentials in educational attainment and the significant educationrelated fertility and mortality differentials that characterize many developing countries, the inclusion of education in population projections significantly impacts population size.

## Political Change

Countries with more educated populations are more democratic, as their citizens are able to make more informed political decisions. The "requisites" of political democratization, education is just one of many factors deemed important. The role of economic factors and noneconomic factors (ethnic heterogeneity, experience with colonialism, religious orientation) as they relate to the rise and stability of democratic institutions.

The positive role of educational expansion in facilitating political development, there are fewer empirical analyses of the impact of educational expansion than there are analyses of these other potential factors. The political modernization perspective sees a strong causal linkage between an educated citizenry and democracy. Schools produce "modern" individuals who have a greater desire and ability to participate in political decisions and national concerns.

People with more schooling tended to be more individualistic, more informed and activist-oriented, and less parochial than those with little education. A longitudinal design through the use of panel data reported more ambiguous results. According to the political modernization perspective, the "aggregate effects of mass education expansion on democracy are largely achieved via education's socializing influences on individuals". Moreover, this view assumes that education has linear effects on individuals that are beneficial for the development and retention of democracy.

The institutional perspective on the relationship between education and democracy differs markedly from that of modernization theory. First, in contrast to modernization arguments, the institutional perspective focuses on the macro-level impact of educational expansion. Educational systems are part of a broader process in the social and political construction of society, in which highly institutionalized social roles and categories are created and legitimated. Thus, educational expansion affects the political development of society not only through its impact on individuals, but also through the wider meanings attributed to given levels of educational attainment.

The "chartering" role of education, and suggests that the organization of education may have as important an effect on political development as the expansion of education. Moreover, whether or not education is beneficial for the development and retention of democracy depends on how educated elites are incorporated into the political system of a nation. In societies where graduates of tertiary education become representatives of the nation-state, the result may be a decline in the independent authority of other collectives.

These perspectives also differ in their views regarding how expansion of different levels of education should influence political development. Political modernization views all levels of schooling as beneficial for the building of democracy, but emphasizes mass schooling - primary and secondary levels as most important. For reasons explained above, institutionalists emphasize the importance of tertiary education.

Both primary and tertiary enrollment ratios have significant, positive effects on both indicators of democracy, with much larger effects at the tertiary level. Educated citizens are more likely to vote and voice more tolerant attitudes and democratic values. The assumption is that schools are responsible for transmitting these outlooks; but exactly how schools promote these outlooks is unclear. Some arguments emphasize curriculum; others stress the institutional influence of the school.

The relationship between education and democracy are noteworthy. First, many of the studies that attempt to measure individual political views and values use paper and pencil tests to determine democratic orientations. It is possible that more educated individuals are better able to guess the "appropriate" answers to questions about political norms. This possibility raises questions about the nature of the relationship between education and political orientations.

Second, the rapid expansion of education in the absence of growth in labor-market opportunities may create a crash in returns to schooling. Certainly the presence of educated, unemployed youth may have a negative impact on political stability. Finally, it is very important to consider the content of education. Similarly, high levels of state control over tertiary education may undermine the support of democratic political institutions because, in such cases, graduates are more likely to become state civil servants and representatives of the nation-state.

# Bibliography


Chomsky, Noam, *Language and mind*, New York: Harcourt Brace Jovanovich, 1968.

Erikson, Erik, *Identity: Youth and crisis*, New York: Norton, 1968.

Gray, Peter, *Psychology*, New York: Worth, 1994.

Maccoby, Eleanor, *The psychology of sex differences*, Stanford, CA: Stanford University Press, 1974.

McShane, John, *Cognitive development: An information-processing approach*, Cambridge, MA: Basil Blackwell, 1991.

Piaget, Jean, *The child's conception of the world*, London: Routledge & Kegan Paul, 1929.

Vygotskii, L. S, *Educational psychology*, Trans. Robert Silverman. Boca Raton, FL: St. Lucie Press, 1997.

Eggen, P., & Kauchak, D., "The teaching of educational psychology: A research agenda", *Paper presented at annual meeting of the American Educational Research Association*, San Francisco,

Huitt, W. (Compiler), *Philosophy and education*, Valdosta, GA: Valdosta State University, 1992, Summer.

Sherman, L., "A post modern, constructivist pedagogy for teaching Educational Psychology, assisted by computer mediated communications", *Paper presentation to the CSCL95 Conference*, Bloomington Indiana, October 17-20, 1995.

Cerbin, W., "Advancing the scholarship of teaching: Pursuing the scholarship of teaching in educational psychology", *Paper presented at the 1999 Annual Meeting of the American Educational Research Association*, Montreal, Quebec, 1999.

Cerbin, W., *A learning centered course portfolio for educational psychology*, Unpublished manuscript, 1992.

Kuhn, D., *A developmental model of critical thinking*, Educational Researcher, 28(2), 16-25, 1999.

Marshall, H., *Teaching educational psychology: Learner-centered constructivist perspectives*. In N.M. Lambert & B.L. McCombs (Eds.) How students learn: Reforming schools through learner-centered education, Washington, DC: American Psychological Association, 1998.

# Index